SIGMUND MOODY

READING PEOPLE

Decoding Body Language, Understanding
Facial Expressions, and Mastering the
Art of Human Interaction
(2024 Guide for Beginners)

Contents

Introduction

The individual qualities that make up who you are as a person pave the way for your personality to develop. With all of the different combinations, you can imagine that each person you encounter on a daily basis has a unique set of behaviors. Broken down into three main categories, a personality revolves around the way that you think, feel, and act. So, what makes for a great personality? A lot of people would agree that those with "favorable" traits such as kindness, compassion, and humor have great personalities. This, however, is subjective. Depending on your own personality, you might perceive others differently.

There is a lot of psychology around the explanation of personalities and the way that we interact with others. Whether you would like to better understand yourself or know why you have a hard time getting along with certain people, being able to identify different personality types is going to be a helpful factor in any social interaction that you have. It can often be a stressful experience when you feel that you are unable to see eye-to-eye with someone, especially if that person is close to you. People can look at the same situation and come to very different conclusions.

Something to remember is that each person is going to have a unique perspective. If you feel that you see something one way and someone else comes along to challenge your views, remember that you might just truly be seeing it differently due to your own unique perspectives. This is why personality types can be so fascinating. Alternatively, you might encounter someone who seems to be on the exact same page. Think about those that you are closest to in your life right now; this bond likely exists because you have similar or agreeable personalities. The term personality stems from the Latin word persona — this refers to a theatrical mask that performers would wear to change identities. These patterns begin developing from the moment that you are born. Early on, your environment has a lot to do with how you choose to behave.

As you can imagine, a child who grows up in a household with loving parents is likely going to have a different personality type than a child who is neglected and left alone. Becoming more impressionable as they grow, children can also develop personalities based on those who they spend the most time around. This is why the parents/guardians and family play such a huge developmental role. The same applies when children begin to make friends and spend time around their peers. While a personality can change and develop over time, there is normally a set foundation of behaviors that remain from early childhood onward.

As children become adolescents, it is not uncommon to experience several different personality changes along the way, only to truly settle in adulthood. This is a very normal part of growing up, and it can often bring out some uncharacteristic behaviors as you try to navigate life as a teenager. It can be a confusing time, especially when you don't exactly understand why you are the way that you are. Many people do not even fully understand personality types well into adulthood, and that is okay. It is a complex topic that does take some research to fully grasp the concept.

Identity

A lot of people will agree that your personality is what makes up your identity. Your identity is how you are known to other people, how others see you. While it is important to have your own opinions about yourself, the way that others perceive you does have the ability to make a difference in how you feel. The way that you identify is important to how you act and react. It is a way for you to feel secure in who you are, and it is through this security that you are able to build up your confidence levels. The more that you are able to recognize these patterns, the easier it will be to understand why people behave the way that they do.

You might be wondering why this is important to learn, and you will find that over time it does make life easier when you have this sense of who people are and even who you are. When you feel comfortable with this concept, you will be able to feel more passionate and secure in your interactions. In turn, this will allow for meaningful relationships and interactions to transpire. It is known that it is human nature to want these types of interactions, whether we realize it or not.

Feeling close to other people can create a very positive and comforting impact on your life. In the realm of psychology, learning about identities and personality types actually makes up for a large branch of study. It shows us just how diverse the human population can be, despite growing up in similar areas or circumstances. There are so many factors that play into your personality, so it can be rather interesting when you decide to look into the way that people begin to form identities. Some are ruled by genetics, while others develop based on situational influences.

Emotional Intelligence

Emotional intelligence is the key to understanding personality types. This is not a conventional skill that can be learned in school or from other people. It is something that must be experienced to be understood. Your emotional intelligence level gives you the capacity to understand yourself and the people around you. It is a way for you to become aware of what is going on around you in order to perceive the behavior that is taking place. As stated, this can be an extremely helpful tool, not only for learning more about other people but also understanding your own personality type. The following are some ways for you to work on your emotional intelligence for the purpose of being able to decipher different personalities:

Giving and Receiving Feedback

An important part of life, being able to handle feedback or critique is an essential aspect of acting in an emotionally healthy manner. Not everybody is going to agree with every single thing that you do, and that is okay. You are also going to have some differing opinions when it comes down to certain behaviors. What we find acceptable or "right" is not always going to be the same across the board. Having a proper amount of emotional intelligence means that you should have no problem giving and receiving this feedback because you see it as a tool that can help you grow as a person. Those who become defensive or angry might have lower levels of emotional intelligence. The more that you are simply able to hear different opinions without becoming reactive will strengthen your ability to grow emotionally.

Accepting Change

Change can be very hard for some people, often leading to debilitating behaviors. In life, nothing is ever going to be certain. There are too many factors resulting in unpredictable results. Having emotional intelligence should make you feel as though you are capable of handling what comes your way. Those who are resistant or unwilling to change will usually have a harder time in life because of this inflexibility. Through learned emotional intelligence, getting used to change will become easier.

Getting Used to Setbacks

Along similar lines of unpredictability, it is not uncommon to experience setbacks in life. No matter how successful or accomplished you become, it would not be wise to assume that you are exempt from failure. It is a normal part of life, and it keeps us humble and grounded. With a strong sense of emotional intelligence, you should be able to learn from your setbacks without allowing them to overcome you. Plenty of people do not know how to react when they are faced with failure. Often times, they will either lash out or simply give up on what they are doing. It does not have to be so black and white; a happy medium can be found in most situations.

Dealing with Challenging Relationships

No matter if the relationship is platonic or romantic, a great way to gauge your emotional intelligence comes from how you interact with other people. Any relationship can prove to be challenging, especially when you take personality types into consideration. Getting into disagreements with those you care about can be taxing and hard, but your actions will reflect your emotional intelligence. Usually, those with a healthy amount of emotional intelligence have no problem with communication and getting to the bottom of a problem. The desire to work out any issues is a great trait to have, but it isn't the easiest to learn.

Handling Deadlines

Mostly applicable in work or school environments, meeting deadlines is another instance when one would need to hone in on emotional intelligence. When stress is added into any equation, it can be easy to crumble under the pressure or blame any shortcomings on those around you. Through emotional intelligence, you should be able to work through this stress in order to accomplish your goals. There is no such thing as stress relief that immediately eliminates all of the stressors, but there are techniques that can be learned in order to efficiently handle what you are going through. Working on your emotional intelligence is something that you can do on a daily basis through very simple actions. For example, during an encounter with another person that you perceive as negative, consider what has caused you to feel this way.

A lot of the time, you might realize that this comes down to their personality and the way that it clashes with your own. You do not need to train yourself to automatically agree with everyone around you, but instead, you can learn how to see things from a perspective that is different from your own. Consider why the other person feels the way that they do; ask them to explain their viewpoints.

When you do this, you are giving the other person a chance to be heard and understood. This tactic normally goes over a lot better than simply shutting the other person down and using conflict to make your point. A lot of people fail to realize that you can have a healthy conversation about differing opinions. This does not mean that an argument needs to ensue or that any negative connotation needs to be used. Instead, the goal should be to come to a point of mutual understanding. If the end of the conversation still results in different opinions, take that for what it is worth.

Use the information to grow and move forward. A big factor that can hinder emotional intelligence is feeling the need to change everyone else's mind. There are a lot of things that you just won't be able to change, but as long as you are using your emotional intelligence to survey and process the information, you are going to continue growing as a person.

Stress Relief

No matter what personality type you have, living a stress-free life is going to enhance all of your best qualities. When you are constantly operating under stress, your actions will reflect this. The way that you treat yourself and other people are impacted by how you feel inside. Imagine how hard it is to be present in any situation when you are worried about something else in the back of your mind. Dealing with stress involves finding outlets for it. The main thing that you should remember is that stress relief will only come from some type of release. While you can form distractions in the moment, unless you are actively working on ways to release the stress, it is still going to remain present. Nobody is immune to the feeling of stress. No matter how old you are or what you do on a daily basis, there is bound to be something that has the ability to stress you out. Being able to deal with stress is an integral part of the human experience. Doing things like taking some time for yourself or sitting with your thoughts can be beneficial to your stress relief situation. When you are trying to work through a tough situation, it is wise to consider the consequences of your actions. In the heat of the moment, you might not be able to think clearly about how you are going to overcome it. The way that you handle things under pressure says a lot about your personality. Much like your emotional intelligence levels, your stress responses can also evolve over time. This is an important thing because it makes you a well-rounded individual. If you are able to recognize your traits and learn how to apply them when appropriate, you will have a better understanding of how to accept yourself and others. Everything makes a lot more sense when you are able to identify it.

Chapter 1: Understanding Personality Types

Considering how many people you have in your life, you can probably think about the differences in behaviors and traits among them all. This can also include your own personality and traits. As expressed, it is a helpful tool to be able to identify and understand many different personality types. Not only does this help you to perceive things clearly, but it also gives you the opportunity to see things from other perspectives. Below are some core different personality groups and traits that go along with them:

Sensing

A person who belongs in this personality group will often be a practical individual. Using the senses means making decisions based on factual information that is reliable. This type of individual is normally very focused on the present and is able to consider the outcomes of problems that they are faced with. Sometimes, a sensing person will not feel secure until there is a clear cut solution to any given situation. Being prepared to handle things is one way that a sensing type is able to feel confident and secure. If approached by a very spontaneous personality type, the sensing individual might feel threatened or not secure with the actions at hand. The best way to interact with a sensing type is to be honest and concise with communication. Giving mixed signals is likely only going to cause the individual to feel as though you cannot be trusted.

Intuitive

An individual who relies on intuition is most likely going to be thinking about the future. Getting a sense of a situation by using gut instinct and then acting is a common method of behavior for the intuitive type. For someone like this, there does not necessarily need to be any concrete information that is needed before making a decision. Gathering context clues from other people, theories, and feelings is what an intuitive type is best at. This person will likely be able to feel at ease by figuring out the situation internally and then taking the result as it comes. If a little bit of mystery is involved, this can sometimes be an exciting aspect to the intuitive type. These people are normally very creative and have active imaginations because they like to utilize those forms of thinking.

Thinking

Arguably the most rational of the personality groups, the thinking type operates exactly as you would expect. Rational thinking is how this type of individual thrives. Being void of feelings to come to a conclusion is typical behavior. That is not to say that a thinking type cannot be emotionally expressive, but that they prefer not to be when it comes to figuring things out. Logic is how a thinking type thrives. Using logical thinking to formulate methods is something that the individual will likely enjoy very much. In the mind of a thinker, there is always a logical solution that can be found to explain any problem.

Feeling

An emotional personality type, a feeling individual is normally very warm and sympathetic toward others. Being able to look at a situation and imagine how others are impacted is a skill that those with empathy are able to accomplish. The feeling type will choose to solve problems by assessing how a situation feels and then determining if it is positive or negative. It is within the feeling nature to want to support other people as best as possible. It can be difficult to see the downfall in other people when it is within the feeling nature to see the best all the time. Imaginably, their traits can be helpful but also hindering.

Normally, when it is being categorized, people will identify as either a sensing or intuition type and a thinking or feeling type. Given all of the different combinations, you can imagine how diverse everyone around you is. When it comes to your own personality, you might find that you identify a certain way at first only to realize that it changes over time. It is interesting to take into consideration what parts of your life might lead you to shift in personality and behavior. It is definitely possible and entirely normal as you grow as an individual.

Personality Types

While you now have a broad sense of some personality types, the categories can be broken down even further. Nobody is simply just going to be one way or the other way because there are so many other factors involved in what makes up a personality. There are several subcategories that can likely be assigned to just about each person you currently have in your life, including yourself. Here are the 16 most common personality types according to Myers-Briggs:

ISTJ (Introverted, Sensing, Thinking, and Judging)

This personality appears to be a bright and logical individual who likes to focus on concrete facts when sorting through situations. They are serious and committed when it comes to relationships and able to stay calm during high-stress situations. Because of their introverted aspect, these individuals are normally on the quiet side, yet they are full of valuable information. Being too social can often feel draining. Due to the fact that they are so detail-oriented, they can be incredibly talented at many different things. Definitely ruled by the head and not the heart, an ISTJ will gravitate toward facts rather than protecting others' feelings. You can expect this person to be very disciplined, hard-working, and prepared for anything.

INFJ (Introverted, Intuitive, Feeling, and Judging)

Gentle and caring, this individual is complex and highly intuitive. Because anything is possible to an INFJ, creativity will be at a high in this personality. Thinking about each situation in a genuine way, the individual can have an uncanny insight. They like to avoid hurting others at all costs, and they can even unintentionally begin to take stress on as their own. This individual is passionate about dreams and ideas, always coming off as approachable. Trusting gut instincts is a common way for an INFJ to sort through things. In this way, the individual will try to make sense of life and what is thrown at them. Organization and creating methods is something that the person truly enjoys doing.

INTJ (Introverted, Intuitive, Thinking, and Judging)

This person is confident and highly ambitious, using bold ideas and complex strategies to navigate through life. They are super intelligent and hold value in their natural state of intuition. A person like this will likely always be thinking about how to make a situation better or how to improve something. Definitely future-oriented, and INTJ can easily see the big picture. They set very high standards for themselves and for their lives, often appearing slightly detached from others. They do value close friendships, though. Surface-level thinking does not necessarily appeal to an INTJ; they would rather be tackling the more complex items that are presented.

ENFJ (Extroverted, Intuitive, Feeling, and Judging)

An extremely giving person, you can expect an ENFJ to be focused on other people. This is a charismatic individual who is outspoken and confident. Being able to connect with others comes naturally to an ENFJ; they rely on their intuition and feelings to do so. This person is highly influential and reliable in all situations. Paired with a warm and caring nature, other people will gravitate toward this individual. They will have difficulty when dealing with the unknown, always preferring to have a plan that is set in stone before proceeding. They are firm in what they believe in, excellent communicators. Because they are so good with people, you can also expect them to be very accepting of all others and genuinely openminded.

ISTP (Introverted, Sensing, Thinking, and Perceiving)

A mysterious individual with a lot of positive qualities, the ISTP operates in a very rational and logical fashion. They are generally very enthusiastic about life, expressing their optimism often. Believing in fairness and equality, the ISTP lives in a practical and realistic type of headspace. They hold a combination of being very easy-going with other people while also remaining confident in their own abilities. The ISTP will enjoy taking risks, despite the way that their logical brain comes forth. This is an independent and determined individual that will observe situations, only to store knowledge for later if needed. The focus remains on the present rather than the future.

ESFJ (Extroverted, Sensing, Feeling, and Judging)

This individual is naturally helpful, sociable, and energetic. They tend to prioritize traditional values, social status, and physical appearance. An ESFJ will jump at the chance to become a role model for someone, enjoying the attention and status. A natural caretaker, you will likely find this individual taking on a leadership role. With a genuine desire to use their skills for the benefit of others, this person is the true definition of a social butterfly. Because of their confidence and compassion, they come across as well-liked and admired. They are always ready to listen to others and to provide advice that stems from warm and genuine thoughts. An ESFJ does not like the thought of uncertainties; they prefer to take control over a situation.

INFP (Introverted, Intuitive, Feeling, and Perceiving)

A deep thinker when it comes to life goals, an INFP will enjoy trying to find deeper meanings behind what they strive for. Through their perfectionist ways, they like to push themselves hard in order to reach their goals. Heavily intuition-based, this individual will use this skill not only in daily life but also when dealing with other people. Generally reserved when it comes to expressing emotions, they genuinely care about others and wish to better understand them. Normally very flexible and laid-back, an INFP will not hesitate to come to the defense of a person or subject that they are passionate about. Despite their introverted nature, they do enjoy being around other people because they are very warm and compassionate.

ESFP (Extroverted, Sensing, Feeling, and Perceiving)

Having strong interpersonal skills is common for an ESFP. They enjoy the spotlight and keep a fun and lively state of being during all situations. This individual is going to be very caring about the well-being of others, and they will show this by using their warmth and friendliness. Living in the present is a must for an ESFP. This is someone who enjoys drama and the excitement of everyday living. They have a natural ability to understand the way that the world operates, making for a grounded sense of being. In their free time, they love to entertain and host others in their homes. You will see that an ESFP appreciates life and all that comes with it.

ENFP (Extroverted, Intuitive, Feeling, and Perceiving)

This is a warm, bright person who is full of potential. No matter what an ENFP sets their mind to, they will likely achieve it with ease because of his initiative. Because of the skills that they possess, it is likely to inspire others along the way. They see the world as blooming with possibilities, and it is within their nature to take hold of them. Surrounding themselves with other people, they truly enjoy the process of getting to know someone. Even with their social nature, an ENFP will not tolerate being controlled or directed by someone else. If given the option, they will spring into the leadership role. Routine tasks are generally perceived as boring; an ENFP enjoys problemsolving tasks.

ESTP (Extroverted, Sensing, Thinking, and Perceiving)

This person will present himself as an enthusiastic and outgoing spirit. They are pretty straightforward individuals that enjoy taking risks in life. While living in the present, an ESTP will likely rely on facts before exploring any theories. They love to have fun, and they love being around other people. When pursuing anything, the ESTP prefers to see instant results rather than waiting around for change. They enjoy risk and adventure, often making them daredevils. Even despite their fleeting nature, they do have a great ability to understand other people and understand other motivations.

ESTJ (Extroverted, Sensing, Thinking, and Judging)

This person will likely be one of the most honest and most dedicated that you meet. Taking pride in hard work is a common trait that is shared between people of this type. A natural-born leader, the ESTJ is organized and likes to take initiative. If there is a difficult problem that must be solved, you can bet that an ESTJ will take charge and go forth in fixing the issue. While some people enjoy change from time to time, this type of individual prefers when things stay the same; they would rather stick to living the same way if that way has been working well for them. This is a responsible person who prefers to plan before acting; a focused type.

ENTJ (Extroverted, Intuitive, Thinking, and Judging)

Seeing challenges as obstacles that can gladly be overcome, an ENTJ enjoys pushing themselves to great lengths. They love to take charge whenever possible, and they enjoy being placed in leadership positions. They have a knack for making careful, yet quick, decisions in the heat of the moment. An ENTJ can absolutely be a bit of a perfectionist at times. Because of how careful and calculated the individual is, their communication skills are one of their strongest traits. This is a confident individual with a logical way of thinking and prefers to stay focused only on the task at hand. Too many outside distractions can be detrimental to the thought process.

INTP (Introverted, Intuitive, Thinking, and Perceiving)

Theories are how the INTP thrives; they love coming up with new ideas that bring forth original thought processes. Normally, this type is very independent. Patterns are easily recognized by the INTP, making them great detectives when it comes to picking out discrepancies. The worst thing that you could do to an INTP would be to lie; that is probably one of the most off-putting qualities to them. Because they are such thinkers, they don't mind sharing thoughts that are not yet fully developed or researched. This is what helps them come to a conclusion.

ISFJ (Introverted, Sensing, Feeling, and Judging)

This individual thrives on giving back to others, a nurturing type. They really appreciate a mutual reciprocation of kindness and generosity. They also tend to be pretty sensitive to the way that others around them feel. Aside from their humanity, they enjoy working hard in a meticulous fashion. This trait often borders the lines of perfectionism. When it comes to responsibility, they like to go above and beyond what is asked of them. They do not need praise or attention, but they simply enjoy serving others. Structure and security are important to an ISFJ, providing some fundamental stability. A sure way to make an ISFJ uncomfortable is to put them in a situation that involves conflict or confrontation.

ENTP (Extroverted, Intuitive, Thinking, and Perceiving)

This is one of the rarer personality types. Even though the ENTP is naturally extroverted, small talk is not desired. An ENTP would rather talk about big ideas or values. They like to be challenged in many ways, finding it thrilling when they are able to find solutions. They can be sweet, loving, and expressive of emotions. This makes it easy for them to form close bonds with their partners and loved ones. Freedom is something that an ENTP holds important, not enjoying when they are controlled by others. You will often find this type of person coming up with new ideas and theories that make you think.

ISFP (Introverted, Sensing, Feeling, and Perceiving)

At first, the ISFP tends to have a hard time connecting to and relating to other people. Because they tend to be pretty quiet and reserved, it does take a little bit of time for them to warm up to you. However, once you break the barrier, they are kind and sweet and care about others' well-being. These individuals are very goal-driven and enjoy coming up with original ideas. They will embrace the chance to experience new things at any given moment. Restrictions make an ISFP feel trapped, so they will do their best to avoid them. Even though they can appear to be incredibly spontaneous on the outside, their inner voice is always one of rational proportions.

Personality and Perception

Research has shown that the way we perceive reality has a lot to do with the way our brains work. Your personality goes hand-in-hand with your thought process, and the same can be said for the way that you perceive others' personalities. While you might see yourself one way for certain, other people might have differing opinions. The science that surrounds this way of thinking is fascinating because it is so diverse. There are no key elements that can be duplicated in order to create two people the exact same way. Even if people grow up in the same environment with the same circumstances, their personalities are likely going to develop differently. The firmest link between seeing situations from the same perspective and thinking the same way lies within the ability to be self-aware. This is something that a lot of different personality types can share, and this is also something that can be worked on. Being self-aware is the ability to understand why you act the way that you do. You can learn this trait by fully understanding your own personality and accepting yourself for who you are. Once you have this grasp on your own personality, you will likely be able to understand others, too. This is why learning about the different personality types is relevant to growing as a person. You will not only gain valuable insight, but you will also become more self-aware in turn.

Chapter 2: Identify Your Personality Type

To find out what type of personality you have, there are certain ways that you can test yourself that will allow you to discover how you operate. Think about the following statements and how they apply to you. Make a checkmark next to each one that you identify with:

1. You are almost never late
2. You like working in a fast-paced environment
3. You enjoy having a lot of acquaintances
4. You feel involved during television shows
5. You are very reactive when things happen
6. You feel that the world is based on compassion
7. You believe that everything in the world is relative
8. Sticking to the rules is likely to hinder a good outcome
9. It is difficult to make you excited
10. When you make a decision, you rely on your feelings first
11. You like to think about our existence and its purpose
12. You believe the best decisions can change situationally
13. You often ponder the root cause of things
14. You prefer to act immediately rather than speculate
15. You trust reason over feelings
16. You are included to rely on spontaneity rather than planning
17. You spend your free time around other people
18. You normally plan things in advance
19. Your actions are influenced by your emotions
20. You are somewhat reserved and distant
21. You know how to use every minute of your time for a good cause

22. You like to contemplate life's complexities

23. After prolonged socialization, you feel the need to be alone

24. You do jobs in a hurry

25. You easily see the principle behind specific occurrences

26. You often express your feelings and emotions

27. You find it hard to speak loudly

28. You get bored when reading theoretical books

29. You tend to sympathize with others

30. You value justice over mercy

31. You like to get involved in the social aspect of a new job

32. The more people you talk to, the better you feel

33. You like to rely on your experience rather than theoretical alternatives

34. You only go forward when you have a clear plan set out

35. You easily empathize with the concerns of others

36. You prefer to read a book than go to a party

37. In a group of people, you enjoy being the center of attention

38. You are more likely to experiment than follow a familiar approach

39. You are strongly touched by other people's stories of hardship

40. Deadlines are merely relative to you

41. You like to isolate yourself from outside noise

42. It is easier for you to learn from a hands-on approach than a book

43. You believe that nearly everything can be analyzed

44. You do not care for surprises

45. You enjoy bringing order to things

46. You feel at ease in a crowd

47. You have excellent control over your temptations

48. It is easy for you to understand new theories

49. You would rather be off to the side than in the center of a room

50. When problem-solving, you prefer to seek a familiar approach

51. You have a thirst for adventure

52. During a situation, you pay more attention to what is current rather than a potential outcome

53. When problem-solving, you consider a rational approach to be best

54. You find it hard to talk about your feelings
55. Your decisions are based on your feelings in the moment
56. You prefer to spend your free time in a tranquil setting
57. You feel more comfortable sticking to conventional ways
58. You are easily impacted by strong emotions
59. You are always looking for opportunities
60. Current problems worry you more than future plans
61. It is easy for you to communicate in social settings
62. You rarely like to deviate from habits
63. You willingly get involved in matters that allow you to sympathize
64. It is easy for you to perceive ways in which events could develop

Once you have thought about your answers, you can find your results at www.humanmetrics.com/cgi-win/jtypes2.asp . The test analyzes your results and places you within one of the 16 different personality types. When you know about the way that you personally operate, you will be able to learn a lot more about yourself. Even those who know themselves well find insight in discovering which personality type they fall under.

Likes and Dislikes

We all have a general idea of what we like and dislike. This is a broad topic, ranging from personal preferences to the activities that we partake in. By understanding the root of where your likes and dislikes stem from, you will likely be able to better understand your decision-making process. While this might not seem important at first, you'll come to realize that you will have a lot more patience with yourself when you fully understand where your thoughts and ideas stem from. It can be hard to accept yourself, especially the qualities that you consider "flaws." Being able to see these behaviors as traits rather than negative qualities can give your self-esteem a muchneeded boost.

When you have confidence, it shows. From the way that you present yourself to the way that you interact with others, going forth with confidence is something that gets you noticed. Even if you don't enjoy being the center of attention, feeling respected is desired by most people. Even as you grow in life and start to make decisions that revolve around your career, knowing about your likes and dislikes is a very helpful tool. You can base your job search on the things that you truly enjoy doing. When you enjoy what you do for a living, it won't end up feeling like work. Also based on what you enjoy doing, you can determine your strengths and weaknesses. This is clearly a great piece of information to know before you put yourself in certain situations.

By knowing your personality type, you will be able to select roles that you feel that you can fill based on your skills. Of course, all of this information about your personality should not limit you. Even if you fit within a certain type, that is not to say that you won't evolve and grow later on.

Introvert vs. Extrovert

You'll notice that the foundation of being either an introvert or an extrovert makes up a large component of your personality type. The concept is relatively simple — introverts feel regenerated after alone time and extroverts feel regenerated after social encounters. Much like a lot of different personality traits, being an introvert or an extrovert can often fall on a scale. Just because you grow up a shy child does not necessarily mean that you will become a quiet adult. As people gain life experience, they have the ability to change and develop new traits.

Social Settings

Introverts: It is a common misconception that people who identify as introverts do not enjoy social interaction. In many cases, these individuals actually do enjoy socializing, but they might feel the need to have less of it than other people. For example, an introvert could enjoy being at a party but will only talk to those that they are familiar with. Staying off to the side or leaving early would also be a common introverted trait that can be recognized.

To an introvert, being around other people is a draining experience. It is not that they do not enjoy the experience, but more that they need time to unwind from it after the fact.

Extroverts: Being around other people is how extroverts thrive. When given the opportunity, an extrovert will choose a situation that allows them to mingle and talk to others. Even in settings that are not as conventional as a get-together, a typical extrovert will normally find it easy to talk to other people in the area. When an extroverted individual is feeling down or uneasy, social interaction is something that they can partake in that makes them feel better. Talking to other people feels like a recharge, an uplifting of the spirit.

Communication

Introverts: Speaking can sometimes cause an introvert anxiety, even if it is a casual situation. There is a correlation between speaking comfortably and self-confidence. Being able to communicate with other people does take some courage, and that is not generally something that comes naturally to an introvert. Though it can be learned, a young introvert might feel uneasy about it at first. In general, you will probably notice that this individual speaks softer and less frequently. The same minimalism also applies to body language; an introvert is not going to be as bold with stance and movements.

Extroverts: Watching an extrovert speak is usually unmistakable. You will notice a lot of direct and lasting eye-contact and a posture that suggests confidence. Aside from enjoying the verbal aspects of communication, an extrovert will also like deciphering all of the non-verbal communication that becomes a part of the conversation. They maintain a strong social presence and are often very memorable. When given the opportunity, an extrovert will most likely be the one who initiates the conversation.

Decision-Making

Introverts: When it comes down to a high-pressure situation, an introvert will probably rely on preliminary information in order to come to a decision. Avoiding rash decisions, an introvert enjoys using thoughtful consideration in their thought process. They will take it upon themselves to make the decision, not usually seeking help from those around them. Intuition is also a skill that is widely utilized by introverts; being able to stop and consider the possibility of any outcome is a very useful trait to have.

Extroverts: If you need someone to make a quick call, you can turn to an extrovert to always have an answer. No matter the situation, an extrovert typically has no problem settling into a decision right away. In contrast to the way that others might approach the situation, an extrovert does not mind guidance when it comes to the decision making process. Hearing advice is something that they actually appreciate and value. Your typical extrovert has no problem stepping back to hear wise words that pertain to the issue.

Workplace

Introverts: Having a quiet workspace keeps an introvert focused. This individual will like to have order and structure to their working life, not leaving room for any distractions that could come along. It is actually thought that introverts react more strongly to noise, therefore causing more disruption when it is present in the environment. When the working circumstances aren't up to par, an introvert is not likely to speak up about them. They prefer to push forward and do the best that they can with what they are given.

Extroverts: An extroverted individual normally perceives work life in a positive manner. Nothing that happens at work normally flows into a person's home life. Being able to keep the two separate is a great trait to have. When it comes to taking action, look no further. At the instance of any type of injustice, you will find that an extrovert has no problem seeking help or authority to get the situation handled. A bustling workplace is not an issue for an extrovert. In fact, the noise is actually quite stimulating to the brain and might help them when they work.

Relationships

Introverts: Just with any other type of social interaction, an introvert is also going to need some alone time within the relationship. To the individual, this is healthy time that definitely should be taken. It gives them the chance to replenish their energy levels and allows them the ability to be able to fully engage with their partner. Because introverts are great with feelings and emotions, they make for very caring partners. When paired with someone who is different from them, introverts will do their best to try and understand the other person to the best of their ability.

Extroverts: When in a relationship, the extrovert places a priority on having fun. This means going out and seeking new experiences while meeting people along the way. An extrovert is sort of like the life of the party, and they like to have their significant other there for it all. Tapping into deep feelings can be a challenge for a taken extrovert. It might take some time or coaxing in order for this type of expression to take place.

Chapter 3: Sensitivity Levels

The topic of sensitivity is often one that comes along with some negative connotations. People who fit the description can sometimes end up feeling that they are inadequate or weak because of this heightened trait. Being sensitive does not simply mean that a person is ill-equipped to handle certain situations. Instead, it indicates that a person is processing things on a different level than what is considered average. It is not a bad thing to be sensitive; this just means that you will likely need to keep in mind that you are going to feel things more strongly than most people. There are definitely ways to be sensitive but also healthy in the way that you navigate through life.

Self-Sensitivity

The way that you perceive yourself is a very important aspect of your personality. If you like who you are as a person, it makes sense that you are going to feel happier and more confident. Being sensitive adds a few challenges when it comes to this self-perception. You might find that you have a harder time letting go of things, whether they are positive or negative. A sensitive type normally chooses to dwell before they move forward. If you have ever found yourself thinking about something that has already been resolved, this might be an indication of your sensitivity. It is also not uncommon for a sensitive type to feel physical ailments that accompany their thoughts.

For example, a sensitive person might have the ability to worry to the point of becoming physically sick. Anxiety is something that can develop in sensitive types pretty easily, so this is why it is important to have an understanding of the topic. Even if you feel that you aren't a sensitive person, it is likely that you have someone in your life who is. Being gentle is the key to avoiding those anxious thoughts. Even during high-pressure situations, if a level of kindness is maintained, it is less likely that the thoughts will evolve into worries. While stress cannot be entirely avoided, the way that you handle it can be adjusted. Needing to punish oneself is also a trait that comes along with being a sensitive person. You might feel mad at yourself for your shortcomings.

The interesting thing is, if another person were in your situation, you would not feel the same way. Being sensitive revolves around feeling inadequate of your own choices and behaviors. You would never judge another person for reaching the same conclusion in the same way. This is an important thing to remember if you feel that you are someone who is too hard on yourself — would you treat your loved one the same way that you are currently treating yourself? Comparison is something that can tend to make you feel like you are not good enough. If you find that you are comparing yourself to others and not allowing for realistic expectations, you might just be setting yourself up for failure. A sensitive individual won't necessarily be able to recognize that these expectations aren't attainable. Seeing this perspective is very important and eye-opening. It is okay to challenge yourself to be better, but also important to remember that you are never going to be a carbon copy of someone else.

Sensitivity with Others

Have you ever been worried about what people think of you as you walk into a room? This is a normal feeling for someone who operates on a high sensitivity scale. Thoughts that can turn into worries about how you are being perceived are common for a sensitive type. Even if the situation does not involve you, you might find that you take things a lot more personally than they actually are. While it is great to be aware of the way that you act and present yourself, you should not allow the fear of not being accepted to hinder you from having certain experiences. This type of behavior directly impacts your confidence levels. When dealing with confrontation, a sensitive person normally finds it hard to let go. Even if the altercation ends on a mutually positive note, the entire event tends to linger in the back of the brain.

There are also certain things that a sensitive type would find triggering that the average person might not. This is another case where you must be kind and gentle with yourself in order to avoid making yourself sick with worry. You must teach yourself that a difference in opinions does not automatically have to result in a screaming match. Accepting criticism (constructive or otherwise) is a tough topic, no matter what the occasion. This type of feedback helps us grow as individuals, but sensitive people have a harder time accepting this type of interaction. To some, this might come across as an insult to abilities rather than helpful advice. This type of criticism can also hit hard when the sensitive individual is in a relationship.

As you can imagine, this can greatly hinder romantic interactions due to the insecurity that comes along with it. Group situations can be tough for a person who is sensitive. Being a part of a group is a common occurrence, from work to social life. Because of the heightened sensitivity, the individual might feel like an outcast even though nothing is apparently wrong. This misconception of not being accepted by others can cause great hindrance in daily life. Due to the fear, the individual might act out in ways that are out of character. This can be awkward and uncomfortable for everyone involved. Alternatively, this can push someone to avoid participating in certain activities for fear of having to face these imaginary judgments.

Environmental Sensitivity

Being sensitive can make everyday situations feel a lot worse than they actually are. For example, crowded spaces can often feel unbearable to someone who operates with higher sensitivity. This type of overstimulation occurs when there is a lot to hear, see, and feel all at the same time. Even things like lights that are too bright and scents that are too strong can trigger something uncomfortable in a sensitive individual. There is really nothing that can be done to avoid these things because they are likely to be encountered on a daily basis. The best way to overcome the feeling is to learn relaxation techniques that force you to focus on only one thing at a time. Environmentally sensitive individuals are also very reactive when it comes to public issues.

For example, this person might feel incredibly distressed upon hearing bad news on television, even if it does not personally apply. Negativity is not something that is taken lightly, and it is very triggering. On a smaller scale, a person could also become upset when scrolling through social media. Seeing negative posts from those around them can sometimes create feelings of negativity in a person's life by association. This is the type of person who does not enjoy anything that one would classify as "shocking" or "appalling." This can all sound detrimental to the person experiencing it, but it is something that the individual gets used to and either works through or suppresses.

Imaginably, this can put unseen stress on a person. Staying happy while being a sensitive individual is all about balance. It is okay to care about what is going on around you, but only to an extent that is healthy. Letting other people's problems take over your own life is not going to benefit you or the other person in any way. It can be hard to remember this when it is your first instinct to want to help others.

Benefits of Being Sensitive

While many tend to focus on the challenges that sensitive people will face, there are truly many benefits. These are some things that you can choose to remember if you find that yourself or someone you care about is in the sensitive category of personality traits:

● **Simplicity is Valued:** To a highly sensitive type, simple interactions mean a lot more than one would think. This person is going to feel happy with genuine conversations and uplifting experiences. There is no need to put on a front when you are in the presence of a sensitive type. Not only will they be able to see right through it, but they also won't find the interaction to be as genuine. Self-care is something that is also highly beneficial and easy to obtain as a sensitive type. If you are sensitive, treating yourself to an activity that you enjoy or even your favorite meal can turn your entire day around.

● **Connections Are Important**: When processing information, those who are more sensitive tend to see details that might become overlooked. This attention to detail can become a valued skill, often providing a whole new perspective to the same old situations. If you find yourself clinging to each little detail, this might work out in your favor. Making connections when given pieces of information is an essential skill. Most people must be taught how to do it, but certain sensitive types just have it in them naturally.

● **Happiness is Attainable:** Being able to appreciate the little things in life paves the way for happiness. To the sensitive one, noticing these things is a main behavioral trait. When you are able to find joy in small nuances, it is easier to stay happy for longer. Those who are sensitive enjoy this quality about themselves, expressing that they don't need many material things in order to reach this level of happiness. It can be a very positive feeling that carries you through your days.

● **Physical Touch is Intense:** Just as emotions are heightened to a sensitive individual, so is physical touch. This doesn't only apply to touch from other people. The feeling can happen when draped in a soft blanket or putting your toes in the sand. Feeling your sense of touch in this way can be overwhelming if you are not used to it. Over time, you will learn to appreciate this part about yourself, realizing that not many people are able to feel the way that you feel.

● **It Is Easy to Judge Character:** Energy is present whenever you interact with another person. Those in tune with this energy can get a feeling of how the interaction is going and what the intentions are. Naturally, being sensitive means having a way with this unique people skill. Those with sensitivity are normally very good at weeding out the good from the bad. This is an extremely beneficial trait, knowing that it can help you from being taken advantage of or lied to. While you might not be able to read minds, being able to read energy is second best.

● **The Body is Sensitive to Substances:** When you drink coffee in the morning, it is meant to stimulate your system in order to keep you going throughout the day. A sensitive individual likely won't need as much caffeine to achieve this feeling. The same can be said for other substances such as alcohol, sugar, and medicine. If you are a sensitive individual, it is important to pay attention to dosage when you partake in any of the above. Because your mind and body feel things more intensely, you will likely need less than the average person.

● **Atmosphere Matters:** Have you ever been somewhere with people that you care about, only to end up feeling uncomfortable? The reason being was probably the unfavorable atmosphere. To the sensitive types, this can be a real deal breaker. Being surrounded not only by the right people but also the right energy, is essential if you are going to be comfortable. Sensitive people truly value a good time that is natural and genuine. Often, distractions and small talk take away from the experience. It doesn't take much to please a sensitive individual, as long as the situation is authentic.

How to Embrace and Understand Sensitivity

With any part of who you are, it is going to take some work in order to fully accept yourself. By learning more about sensitivity, you might find that you fit into this category perfectly. There is no clear-cut way to just simply accept who you are overnight; it takes a lot of self-love and self-care. Don't be afraid to spend some time alone, just doing things that you genuinely enjoy. It is much easier to be accepting of yourself when you are in the mood to do so. By opting for activities that bring out the best in your personality, you are naturally going to be happier and more relaxed. Try your hand at journaling. You might not know what to say at first, but if you just try putting pen to paper, you could be surprised at what thoughts spring to mind. Do your best to not "censor" your personality or who you are. If you realize that you know some sensitive people, then the same general principles apply. Talk openly with your sensitive loved ones and support them by providing a listening ear when needed. Remember, those who are more sensitive truly appreciate genuine interaction. It doesn't take much to make a positive impact. If you are ever in a situation where you notice that the other person is feeling uncomfortable, do your best to create a better atmosphere. While there is only so much that you can do from the outside, your effort can make all the difference.

Chapter 4: Types of Temperament

When describing your temperament, it is easiest to explain it as the core factor that drives your behavior. This is something that is with you from the moment that you are born, and it is unlikely to change very drastically over time. Though it can fluctuate based on the circumstances, your temperament is normally a permanent part of who you are as a person. This is a very big part of all that makes up your personality. There are various components that make up a person's temperament. For example, someone can be introverted, withdrawn, and very reactive — this is likely going to be a more difficult temperament. On the complete opposite end of the spectrum, one can be adaptive, easy-going, and calm. The possibilities are endless, and the results are able to be psychologically charted.

As a child, it is normally very easy to understand temperament; you either have a fussy baby or you don't. While it isn't exactly this black and white, it is a lot more simple in young people. Paying attention to an infant's crying habits is one of the easiest ways to monitor temperament. Does the baby cry throughout the night? Is it hard for you to get him to stop crying? Whether the answer is yes or no, there is no such thing as a perfect temperament. Much like any other personality traits, there are benefits that can be found no matter what.

Aside from crying, you can monitor how often a baby smiles when you are trying to determine temperament. Is it easy or hard to make the baby smile? Judging by these patterns, you should be able to loosely predict what the future temperament is going to be like. Of course, your main goal with infants is to keep them smiling as much as possible. A healthy and loving environment is going to attribute a lot to the future of their temperament. Things stay pretty easy when babies are able to stay in controlled environments.

Temperament Through Childhood

Genes play a huge role in the temperament of a child. If the family is known for happy babies who hardly ever cry, you can expect this pattern to continue. Of course, not all families are this fortunate. This is not a negative aspect because outlook can be everything. As a child grows, even despite having a difficult temperament, the behavior can be curbed by positive reinforcement. This means showing the child as much love as possible and introducing a stable environment from early on. Maintaining this consistency is important when it comes to influencing temperament. If the environment is ever-changing, it is unlikely to make a difference in temperament.

In addition to environmental needs, parenting also plays a major role. The parent(s) should be able to form a distraction during times of distress. Any type of parenting techniques that seem to focus on what is distressing can be traumatic in the long run. Being present is also very important. A child is not going to know how to express emotions unless you lead by your own example. Allow for this healthy expression often, showing the child that it is okay to feel many different ways. Stress is going to eventually become a part of every single person's life. It is unavoidable, but whenever possible, keeping a child away from what could potentially become stressful will drastically help with temperament. A child should not be left to worry about issues that they cannot change.

If you are a parent, do your best to create a gentle buffer between your child and any stressors. This is not to say that you need to pretend that everything is always okay — things happen. It's normal. Create a realistic approach that you can abide by in front of your child.

How to Curb Temperament

When it comes to making a big change, smaller steps should be sought out. Whether it is to curb the behavior of a child or to make a life change as an adult, the root cause of temperament should always be taken into consideration. If you are looking to make a change for yourself, think about all of the reasons why. Acknowledge that there are parts of yourself that need improvement, parts that you would like to work on. Know that you are still a whole and functioning person, even despite these things that you do not love about yourself. It is never too late to make a change, as long as you are willing to put in the work that comes along with it. To start, make a list of some goals that you would like to accomplish. Maybe you would like to work on your anger management skills.

If you find yourself often having uncontrollable outbursts, figure out ways that you can calm yourself down before you end up reaching that point. Perhaps you would like to become less reactive to situations that do not directly impact you. If you are a sensitive person, this can be incredibly hard. Letting go is one of the most challenging steps to moving forward in life. Consider ways that you can deal with all of the emotions that you have that surround each situation. No matter what you need to work on in order to better your temperament, there is always an attainable solution. What do you do if you notice that someone in your life could use some help with their own temperament? You must start by realizing that no one is going to change unless the change comes willingly. No matter how great you think your advice is, nobody is truly obligated to take it unless they feel that they connect with it. The best thing that you can do for other people is to set a great behavioral example. If you notice that your friend is struggling with gossiping about other people, try to change the topic of conversation to something that is more positive and fulfilling. Small steps such as this can make a big difference in the lives of others.

Most Common Temperament Types

There are 4 primary temperament types that have been identified by professionals. These studies were done based on the way that the brain processes information. While the different types are general behavioral guidelines, an individual might have a few combinations that make up the totality of their personality.

Sanguine

The most common of all types, it is a people-oriented temperament. This individual should have no problem talking to and interacting with others. Found equally among men and women, this type is the epitome of outgoing and sociable. They love to help others and enjoy the opportunity to take on leadership roles. They have the ability to express a wide range of emotions. If a change is needed in their own personal environment, a Sanguine type should be perfectly capable of making that change. This is a person that has the ability to be playful and even impulsive. You will find that they are easily amused and capable of entertaining those around them.

When interacting with someone who has a Sanguine type temperament, you might feel as if you have known this person for a very long time, even if you are just meeting, They have an uncanny ability to build strong relationships with other people. You will likely feel comfortable talking to them by default. Because this individual has little to no filter, their actions might lead to disarray. They must try hard to stay focused at all times. If there is any type of competition, a Sanguine type is going to want to win. It doesn't matter if it is within sports, politics, or business, this individual will make it a point to get noticed. Combined with the effortless social skills, this is a person who normally holds a lot of self-confidence.

Phlegmatic

Also a common temperament, this is almost the direct opposite of Sanguine. Though the two are very different, it is still possible for a person to have one as their primary and the other as their secondary. This is an individual that chooses to be service-oriented. Even though they are introverted, they still enjoy working together or for others to accomplish a common goal. During group settings, they tend to be passive, allowing others to take the lead. They can be great followers. This is a person known for being super calm in all situations; you won't find a Phlegmatic type acting out in emotion. This level-headed quality will come in handy several times throughout a person's life. Though they can sometimes be indecisive, they normally have no problem with someone else stepping in to give them advice or even make decisions on their behalf. In regard to other people, it can take the Phlegmatic type a little bit of time to warm up to you.

Once this barrier is broken, they are able to easily make new friends and build relationships. This is by far one of the easiest types of temperament, rooted in the act of patience. They do not care for change and will likely stick to the same routine for a very long time. Daily life is normally centered around family life and home life. They would rather spend their free time at home with those who mean the most. No matter what happens in their loved one's lives, a Phlegmatic type is going to remain loyal. This is one of their strongest traits. When something goes wrong in a relationship and the trust is broken, you likely won't find the individual returning to it.

<u>Melancholy</u>

Upon hearing the word, you might be reminded of a person who is constantly feeling down. By temperament terms, a Melancholy type is actually someone who prefers to act cautiously. This individual is extremely detail-oriented and tends to be very observant. Their main goal in life is to find what is "right" and they can sometimes be perfectionists about this. Through and through, a Melancholy individual is a follower. They believe that rules exist for a reason and are not meant to be bent or broken. In unfamiliar situations, you can expect a Melancholy individual to approach cautiously. When something becomes truly unfavorable, you might see their defense mechanism of aggression come into play.

These individuals are very private and will act extremely introverted. They are ruled by logic, often analyzing a situation thoroughly before acting upon it. In order to keep anxiety at bay, the Melancholy type must have a solid plan for everything that they do. They feel at ease when there are clear steps to follow. Regarding their anxiety, a Melancholy individual does worry about what other people think. They also express guilt at high levels if they are ever unsure about their own actions.

A Melancholy individual is never late for an appointment and tends to keep things extremely organized. They will often ask very specific questions in order to gain enough information that they are comfortable with. When it comes to trusting other people, you will have to work hard in order to be approved by someone of Melancholy temperament. They tend to generally be suspicious of others until proven otherwise. For this reason, it can be more difficult for them to form long-lasting relationships. When a relationship is formed, they are going to hold it to a very high standard.

Choleric

This temperament is the rarest of all 4. More specifically, females with this type as their primary are incredibly rare to find. The Choleric type is generally seen as a secondary temperament. This individual is resultsoriented, seeking plenty of goals to reach in everyday life. Driven toward success, you will likely find a Choleric type in a positive state of mind with the desire to continually move forward. When faced with any type of opposition, they confront it head-on in order to maintain their desired results. A Choleric individual will appear very extroverted and self-confident. When given the choice, they prefer to do things on their own. This independent trait makes for a very strong-willed person. When they communicate, they prefer to be very direct with their intentions. There is no beating around the bush for a Choleric individual; they mean exactly what they say. Some people might come to the conclusion that the individual is a little bit rude because of how direct they are. When it comes to relationships, a Choleric person can tend to be a little bit controlling. Since they are fiercely independent, there might be a bit of a double standard in love.

This person is going to do exactly what they want, no matter what. Getting bored pretty easily, you can almost guarantee that a Choleric person will enjoy taking many risks. When it comes to decision making, they will not only have no problem making their own decisions, but also decisions for other people. As you can imagine, they do enjoy being in a leadership role rather than a follower role. These individuals can be very creative and generally have a vision for their plans before beginning. They operate in a practical manner, never cracking under any form of peer pressure. While they are able to show compassion, it does take a Choleric individual some time to slowly build up meaningful relationships. It does take a while for them to get angry, but once they are in this mood, it can be very difficult for them to shake the feeling.

Chapter 5: Personality Comparison

While there are several different personality types, a lot of them have certain similarities. Taking a look at them on a comparative level, you will see that there are traits that tend to repeat themselves. Below are some charts to utilize for comparative purposes. You can take a look at them to better understand the way each personality type operates.

<u>Introverts and Extroverts</u>

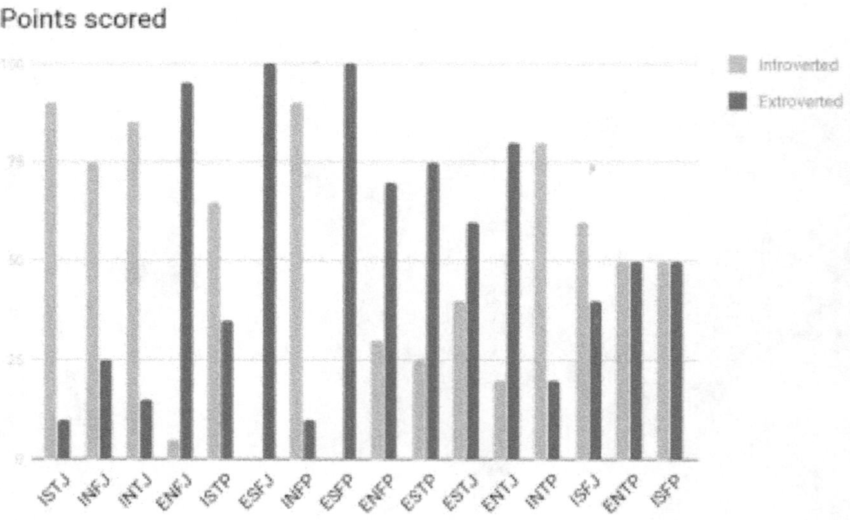

<u>The 16 Personality Types Compared by Introverted and Extroverted Behaviors</u>

Taking a look at the above chart, you can see that there is quite a bit of diversity among all of the personality types. Just because your personality type begins with a letter "E" does not necessarily mean that you do not have any introverted qualities, and vice versa. This is a common misconception that people have when they are trying to learn about these personality types. Coming in at the most introverted, you will see that ISTJ, INTJ, and INFP have the most introspective qualities. Even though they have very similar levels of introverted behavior, you can see that all of them vary in extroverted behavior. An ISTJ individual will likely never make the first move when it comes to being social. They can do alright in a social setting, likely keeping to oneself the entire time. The only way that you would see an ISTJ being social is probably when someone else makes the first approach. For an INTJ, the balance is a little bit different.

While they are still individuals that do enjoy being alone to recharge, they also have slightly more of a desire to be social. This person might like to go out from time to time, but it definitely will not be their most favorite way to pass the time. Extroverted desires might appear very rarely in this personality. An INFP will operate pretty similarly to an ISTJ. They have proportions that nearly mirror one another. Arguably, an INFP is less intense and less passionate.

Next, take a look at ESFJ and ESFP — neither one has introverted aspects. These are definitely the most social of all the personality types, showcasing their desires to gain attention and notoriety by their actions. Though they both enjoy being around other people, they will express it in different ways. An ESFJ will join groups and organizations, boosting their popularity through what they decide to do in life. An ESFP loves to be the center of attention, never hesitating if given the opportunity to perform. They are the logic and creative of the extroverted personalities. A unique duo, ENTP and ISFP share one thing in common. They both have equal aspects of being introverted and extroverted.

The main difference is the way that they decide to portray their actions. An

ENTP enjoys mental stimulation. This individual will seek out ways to learn and grow mentally. An ISFP enjoys exploring many different situations and putting themselves out there. This doesn't always necessarily mean that they are going to be in the foreground of the action, though. They do not mind tagging along and watching other people have the experiences.

Sensing and Intuition

The second letter of each personality type has to do with either sensing or intuition. This is the way that we perceive situations and then make a decision on how best to act. A person who relies on sense focuses very much on the present time. They generally do not consider what the past or the future has to offer. The intuitive type tends to use their creative side when it comes to making a decision. They will consider all possibilities, even ones that are more unconventional. While a personality type mainly contains either one or the other, here is a breakdown of how each type utilizes their sensing and intuition.

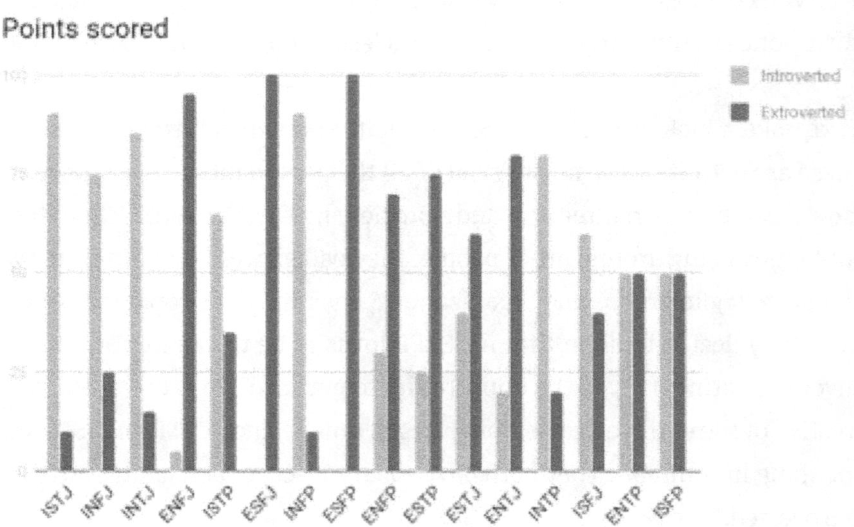

<u>**The 16 Personality Types Compared by Sensing and Intuitive Behaviors**</u>

At first glance of this chart, you can see how there is rarely a tie between sensing and intuitive behaviors. The only personality type that tends to utilize an equal amount of both is the ISFP. This is an introverted sensing sign that does not act like the typical traits that it encompasses. Because they enjoy embracing the present, this gives them their sensing title. However, they are also able to think in abstract terms, relying on their intuition to get them through certain situations. This is a widely versatile personality type that is full of unique behavioral traits.

ISTJ and ESTP are firmly rooted in their sensory behavior. These are two personality types that prefer to think only about the information directly in front of them. It does not make any sense for them to consider future outcomes or past influences. On the complete opposite end of the spectrum, you have ENFJ and INFJ. Thinking creatively is what both of these types excel at.

In fact, ENFJ does not even contain any sensory thinking habits at all. These individuals are strongly rooted in their intuitive behavior. Each letter of the personality type makes up for a portion of how the individual behaves. As you can see, even if a person is a strong extrovert, they can also be intuitive thinkers. Because there are endless possibilities, it can be hard to predict exactly how somebody is going to operate. Learning about all of the personality types will help you know more about yourself and also know how best to interact with other people in your life. Using the charts as references, you can get a basic idea of what it means to be each different personality type.

Feeling and Thinking

These two traits can be compared to being right brained or left brained. A feeler is normally someone who can think creatively, using imagination in order to fill in the blanks about the unknown. A thinker likes to consider things carefully, making sure that they have logic on their side before making any decisions.

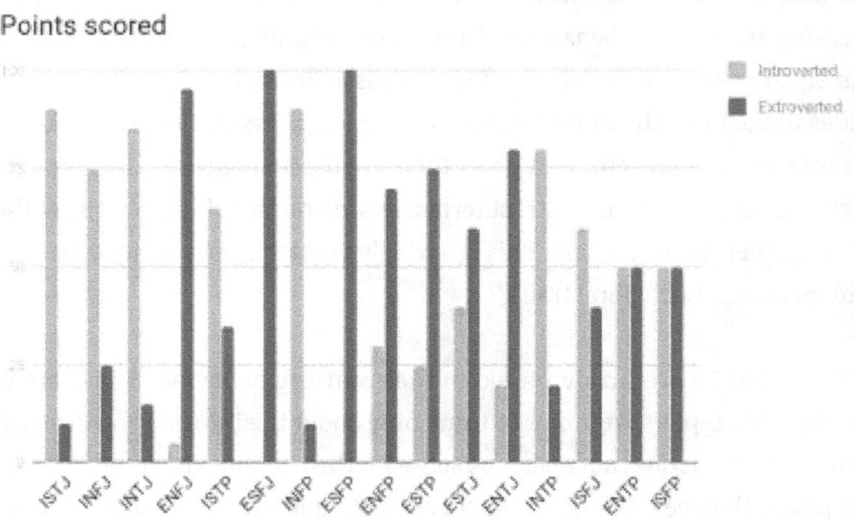

<u>The 16 Personality Types Compared by Feeling and Thinking Behaviors</u>

One of the very first things you'll probably notice is the direct opposition between INFJ and INTP. Respectively, each one solely focuses on either feeling or thinking. When it comes to the way that we do or do not include our emotions in any given situation, the methodology is normally pretty black and white. Some people prefer to only stick to the known facts, while others have no problem subbing in information that comes from different feelings. The INFJ and INFP are relatively set in their ways. They do not need to utilize both behaviors because they are both personality types that find comfort in sticking with something that works. You will also notice that there are several types that see things from a 50/50 point of view. These are ESFJ, ENFP, and ISFP.

Generally, all 3 of these personality types are generally pretty agreeable people. They normally have no problem with going with the flow and taking life as it comes. All of them are able to see the value in thinking logically about a situation while also considering that there can be several unknown outcomes just lurking around the corner. Because these types are so balanced, they will also have an easier time understanding other people that are around them. The rest of the personality types seem to follow a similar pattern across the board; they typically utilize their named trait as their main one, but they do have the ability to see the other side of things if need be.

The ability to remain flexible during times of decision-making is important. If you are too rigid in your ways and viewpoints, you are likely to butt heads with other people. You also might find that you are too stubborn to successfully move forward because of your inability to make some alterations to your behavior. If you find that your personality type leans too far one way for your liking, you can exercise your ability to try and change the way that you think. This is a healthy exercise for every personality type to partake in from time to time.

Judging and Perceiving

The judging type tends to be very meticulous and organized in their thought process. They do not participate in things without giving 100%. When these individuals feel that are well-established and orderly, they can perform at their best level. Perceiving individuals have no problem acting spontaneously. They are alright with putting the decision-making on hold until they are satisfied with all of the options that they have in front of them. A perceiving type is not bothered by having unresolved situations. They also do not mind making last-minute decisions.

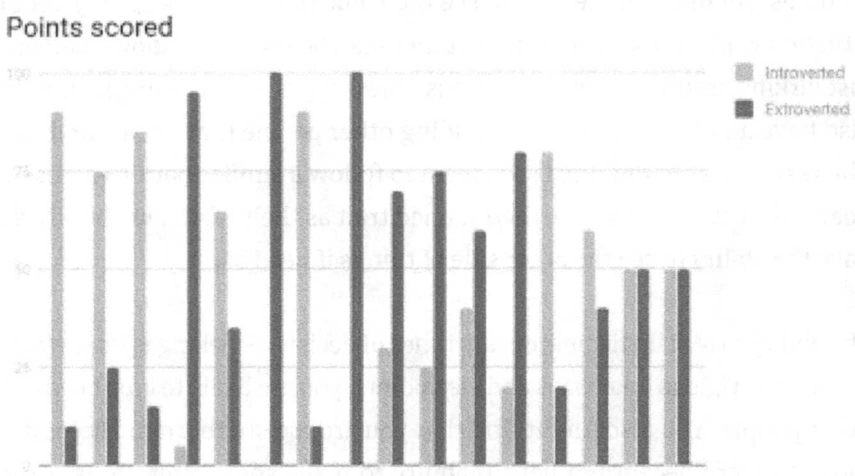

The 16 Personality Types Compared by Judging and Perceiving Behaviors

In this example, INTJ and ESFP are mirror images of one another. The former is all about coming to an orderly conclusion in a way that makes sense to them. While you can try to give them outside advice or suggestions, it is unlikely that they will waiver. The latter is a free spirit, the definition of the title. They prefer to spontaneously come to their conclusions based on what feels right in the given moment. While neither one of these traits is better than the other, you can see how differently the two can operate when faced with the same situations. ENFJ, ESFJ, and ENTP are all personality types that can waiver in their behavior. There is not a strong need for either judging or perceiving in order to come to a satisfactory conclusion. These individuals are likely the ones who are okay with advice that is given to them. Depending on if the advice speaks to them, they may or may not take it. The point is that they are the most flexible of all the personality types when it comes to the judging and perceiving traits. Seeing all of the different personality types in action really puts into perspective the fact that we all view the world differently. We all have different perceptions of ourselves and the environment that we exist in. Just because two people have grown up under the exact same circumstances does not necessarily mean that they will turn out the same way. The personality type and temperament have a great deal to do with the final version of one's personality. If you have ever thought that it was impossible to figure someone out, maybe you aren't looking at the big picture. This logic can also help you when you are feeling unsure about your own behaviors. These charts shed a lot of insight into why we all are the way that we are.

Chapter 6: Personality and Love

Love is something that can make anyone act out of the ordinary. We feel things more intensely and even see things differently when we are in love. Taking a look at how each personality type handles relationships can explain a great deal about your past, present, and future romances. In general, if you have a fairly easy-going personality with a fun-loving attitude, it is safe to say that you will likely have positive experiences during most relationships that you can encounter. What can often set the balance off is what type of personality your partner has. When you bring two people together in such an intimate way, it is likely that certain behaviors will surface that you might not even realize existed. Overcoming differences while in love can be a challenge because your brain might be clouded with feelings. Depending on how you are able to perceive things, it might be a little bit hard to differentiate what is factual and what is emotional.

There are some people that have no problem doing this, and can actually have the ability to push it too far. Being distant from your partner can cause just as many issues as being overly expressive. Love takes balance from both parties involved, and you are not going to be able to accomplish this fully unless you both have an accurate understanding of how each other operates.

<u>Compatibility Check</u>

When you are in a relationship with someone, it is important to find out if you are both compatible with one another. There is a difference between compatibility and attraction. You have probably experienced certain instances when you fall very quickly for someone, only to find out that you actually have nothing in common. A lot of people discover this the hard way, dating the "wrong" person for months or years at a time, only to eventually realize that they aren't compatible in the slightest. This can make the task of finding someone to date seem daunting. While you don't have to agree on every single thing, it does help when you share the same basic values and interests.

What are some behaviors that you deem unacceptable? It is important to have this established in your mind before you set out on the dating scene. If you meet someone who happens to display this behavior over time, you will find yourself in a tricky situation. Stand firm in what you believe in, speaking up about what you find off-putting. What are some things that your partner must possess? For some, it is a great sense of humor. For others, it is the ability to openly communicate. This is going to vary depending on the person, but in dating, all of your preferences are valid.

Remember, the person you date is someone that you are going to likely be spending the majority of your time with. You need to make sure that you align in viewpoints. Having differences is not a deal-breaker by any means. It is healthy for couples to be individuals. This is what keeps a relationship strong — two separate people that come together based on commonality and attraction. If you and your partner align in the essential ways but not in what you find fun and exciting, this is okay. Being with someone who is a little bit different from you can bring out some new aspects to your personality and vice versa. This type of relationship will challenge you to become a more open person, encouraging you to try new things.

Consider how your partner feels in social settings. This is not only an important aspect of dating but also of life in general. There are going to be many opportunities where you will find yourself in social scenarios. If you are on the introverted side, being with another introvert might make you feel as though you have an alliance. It will be like dating a person who can relate to you when it comes to socialization. Alternatively, if you are an introvert who is dating an extrovert, your partner might push you to come out of your shell. A little bit of healthy socialization can be great for keeping your personality balanced. You know what they say, opposites attract. As long as you are comfortable with what is going on, then you know that you and your partner are likely compatible

Overcoming Differences

When you enter a relationship with someone, you are going to have to learn how to work through your differences. Some can be minor things, such as disagreeing on what to watch at the movie theater and deciding on where to go for dinner. Other things might hold a more serious weight. One of the number one things to tear a relationship apart is a lack of communication. If you do not communicate with your partner, you cannot expect them to read your mind and know exactly what you want. Speaking up can be hard, especially for those with regressive personality types. It might almost seem easier to go with current events and be agreeable than to trigger a potential confrontation. While this might be true, just know that the issue will still persist even when you choose to ignore it. This is why some couples will go for a long time without having a fight and then an explosive one occurs that is filled with all of the suppressed tension.

Consider the following ways that you can work on overcoming your differences with your partner:

● Have Alone Time: Take a designated slot of time each week to just spend some time alone with your partner. You will never be able to work on your problems if you are constantly surrounded by friends and family. Always have serious talks with one another in your own company, if possible. Having other people around for the discussion can make things complicated and messy. Your personal business should stay between the two of you. This is one way to make sure that the situation is unbiased and not influenced by outside sources.

● Focus on Commonalities: When you spend time with your partner, try to do something that you both enjoy. If both parties feel that there is equality in the relationship, then there will be less need for bickering. Of course, you do not have to do every single thing with your partner. If you love ice skating but your significant other does not, choose to go skating with your friends instead. Simple changes like this can show that you are considerate but also allow you to do all of the things that you want to do.

● Think Before Speaking: A lot of couples launch into discussions that eventually turn into heated arguments. As a good rule of thumb, do not begin discussing a problem until you are absolutely certain that you know what you want to say. This can be hard, especially for those outspoken personality types. Having a clear head with save you from unnecessary fighting, though. Think about how you are feeling, sans the opinion of your partner. After this, determine what is causing you to feel that way. Finally, take a look at the big picture and how this impacts the relationship. Taking these few moments to gather your thoughts can help with altercations that arise.

● Seek Therapy: Getting rid of the notion that seeking help is a negative thing can really change the quality of your relationship. Plenty of couples seek professional help during many stages of a relationship. Going to a therapist is kind of like having a mediator available during your discussions. Some couples appreciate having this additional viewpoint to assist with getting through the tough challenges. While therapy isn't for all couples, if you feel that it might even slightly benefit you, do not be afraid to try a session. A therapist is professionally changed to recognize different personality types and to have a better understanding of what kind of techniques will work best.

Personality Positives

With all of the focus on how different personality types can hinder relation-ships, there is always the opposite view — some personality traits enhance your love life. If you are someone who enjoys helping other people, think about all of the ways that you can make your partner happy. A lot of individuals enter relationships because they want to be taken care of, whether that be physically or emotionally. A lot of personality types include that caretaker trait; it is one that brings great comfort to other people. Being a caring type brings a sense of stability into the relationship. It makes you a reliable person that your partner can count on. Those who love to speak up can also make great partners. If you are extroverted and enjoy launching into discussions, then you have a lot to offer another person. Being with someone who isn't afraid to speak their mind can be a very positive quality.

A lot of people forget that change begins within, and no one is going to initiate the change unless you start. An extroverted partner with a need for justice is a go-getter in the romantic world. This type of individual is normally very clear and concise with thoughts. Being agreeable does not necessarily mean that you are going to get walked all over. Dating someone who identifies as agreeable means that you are with someone that is flexible with change. Because relationships are often filled with many unpredictable changes, this is an important quality to possess. A partner who is agreeable is not weak. In fact, this person is quite the opposite. Being able to set your pride aside and adapt to a change is a personality trait that is extremely useful to have. Relationships containing at least one agreeable partner keeps things running smoothly.

The way that a person thinks contributes a lot to a relationship. Someone who can see logic and reason in situations will normally have a very rational approach to finding a solution. This type of person remains rooted in the present, preferring to think about the outcome of the given situation. On the other end of the spectrum, those with the ability to think abstractly have open minds about tough situations. These individuals choose to see solutions as plentiful and unique, considering what will happen not only in the present but also in the future. As you can see, this is all about perspective. Even when two people are in one relationship and dealing with the same issues, there can be very different methods to approach problemsolving.

How to Be Harmonious

So you've identified your personality type, and you know how your partner operates. What can you do to keep the relationship harmonious? A common misconception is that you must change yourself in order to be more like your partner or what your partner needs. As previously discussed, this all goes back to the compatibility factor — it should come naturally. If you find that you are changing who you are as a person solely for the sake of a relationship, then maybe you need to evaluate why you are doing this. Your connection with your partner should feel strong and secure, regardless of your behavioral habits. You should both feel comfortable talking with one another and enjoy spending time together.

If a problem does arise, do not sweep it under the rug. This is when you must work on yourself in order to better your relationship. Speak up about any feelings that you are having and work on sorting through any tension before it becomes a bigger issue. In this instance, you need to be mindful that your partner might have a different way of dealing with the problem. Encourage openness and show that you are willing to talk about things in a non-confrontational way. Couples who choose to communicate from the beginning can often avoid those arguments and the bickering that follows. Space is a great thing. Couples who never take time to apart tend to argue more frequently.

Consider what you have learned about introverts and extroverts — depending on what you need, take your time to recharge. This can mean having lunch out with friends or spending some time alone reading books. It is not wrong to express these needs to your partner, because more often than not, they will also need their own time to recharge. As cliche as it sounds, distance does make the heart grow fonder. Remember why you fell in love. Another cheesy sentiment, but thinking back on what brought the two of you together can help to reignite some positive feelings.

Relationships take work, especially when you have two different personality types coming together. Getting back to your roots will not only make you happier as a couple, but it will also remind you of the ways that your personality types work well together. Many people tend to forget the little things as they stay in the relationship over time. This is very normal, and all it takes is a little bit of effort to get back to that happy place. Even if you are not the initiative type, try branching out of your comfort zone in order to make this happen for your relationship.

Chapter 7: Personality and Emotions

Emotions go hand-in-hand with your personality. These feelings arise from your mood, environment, and relationships. It is entirely normal to feel emotions; some people feel them more intensely or more often than others. There are different levels to emotions and unique ways that they can form depending on your personality type. What is important to remember is that emotions don't just formulate out of nothing. They are a triggered response to situational stimulation. For example, if you find yourself watching a sad movie and you begin to cry, you'll notice that your emotions are highly active. Being able to not only accept your own emotions but be understanding other people's emotions, is a key to understanding different personality types.

7 Common Emotions

Human emotions can be complex and unpredictable at times, but it is important to remember that they normally stem from one of the following that are most commonly felt:

Anger

We are all familiar with the feeling, both stemming from our own feelings and from others'. Even though being angry has a negative connotation, it is still an important emotion that needs to be felt from time to time. Knowing that you feel angry means that you can acknowledge that something is not right. The way that you choose to deal with this anger speaks volumes about your personality type. Ideally, we want to feel the emotion before eventually moving forward and finding a solution to what is causing the anger.

Understandably, some people have a hard time letting go. Because anger is such an intense emotion, it does take a lot of effort to move past it. How We Express It: Anger presents itself pretty clearly when it comes to body language. You will notice a change in the eyebrows and eyes, a tightened lip position, and potentially even a rigid demeanor throughout the entire body. These physical traits of anger are meant to show others that we are strong and protected. Even within the most gentle personality types, you will see anger as an emotion that creates an invisible shield around a person.

Fear

This is the emotion that appears before your fight-or-flight response kicks in. We all have different things that make us scared, but the way that we express fear can differ greatly. Some personality types refuse to show weakness, therefore pretending that they are not afraid of anything. Others have no problem allowing the fear to take over. There is no right or wrong way to deal with this emotion, as it is very complex. The one thing that you can work on is handling how you first react to situations that induce fear. Staying calm is the key. How We Express It: When fear is present, a person will normally show this directly through their eyes. They will appear wider with raised eyebrows. The mouth might naturally fall open slightly, with the breath being held. If breathing is occurring, it is normally at a quicker rate than normal. The stance that is taken can be compared to that of a deer in the headlights, trying to decide what will be the smartest next move.

Disgust

This emotion can often be perceived as rude by other people. Showing disgust means that you truly do not enjoy what is being presented to you or what is occurring around you. Again, depending on the personality type that you have, the way that you act on disgust can look diverse. Those who are more shy will deal with the disgust on their own time. This type of individual will likely hold onto it longer, thinking back on it. People who choose to handle things more directly might approach disgust in a confrontational way.

How We Express It: A wrinkled nose is a key giveaway to a feeling of disgust. You might find that the upper lip is pulled up, even wrinkled. The eyebrows will naturally pull themselves down. These responses are all natural because they were meant to protect us. Whether it is a sight, sound, or smell that we find disgusting, closing off our bodies prepares us to tackle the issue.

Happiness

This is one emotion that most of the personality types tend to express in the same fashion. Happiness is a joyous emotion that can present itself in many different ways. You can be happy about something that is going on in your life, you can be happy with yourself, you can be happy for other people, and you can even be indirectly happy (think about watching your favorite characters on TV). It is one of the most common human emotions that gets expressed on a daily basis.

How We Express It: The number one indication of happiness comes from a smile. Ironically, researchers believe that our smiles actually came from the desire to show our teeth and assert dominance. In today's society, it has evolved into a lovely form of self-expression. The eyes also appear warmer when happiness is being expressed, sometimes even becoming squinted. There is a reason why people say that happiness is the most universal emotion. It is so easily recognized by all.

Sadness

Of all the emotions, this is arguably the most complex. Though it is normal to feel sadness, the ways that we express it are vast. Some personality types find it very hard to get into this vulnerable state of being, avoiding sadness like the plague. Others cannot help but succumb to sadness, allowing it to take over. It is uncommon to have a middle ground when it comes to experiencing sadness; you either feel it or you don't. This is another emotion that greatly relies on proper handling in order to move past it. Finding healthy ways to vent becomes essential to anyone who is going through something hard or depressing.

How We Express It: Crying is a very normal response to sadness. If actual tears do not fall, the eyes tend to well up with them. Lips begin to quiver, the corners being pulled down. The inner corners of the eyebrows raise ever so slightly. Sadness has a few very slight physical details that are important to recognize, even if the person is not crying. This helps you when you are trying to understand others. If you can detect sadness without being told about it, then you are likely going to be a person who is trustworthy enough to provide help working through it.

Surprise

It is a fast-acting emotion that can either come from something that is very positive or very negative. This is a hard emotion to fake. Being surprised is actually a desired emotion by some. Those who seek it enjoy the feeling of losing control for those few seconds. Imaginably, this loss of control can sometimes cause people to feel scared or uncertain. If you have ever wondered why you either love or hate surprises, then this might provide you with some insight. Each person has different ways of processing and working through the emotion of surprise.

How We Express It: If you take a look at a person's eyebrows, you will be able to indicate if they are feeling surprised. The entire eyebrow area will be lifted, likely causing the forehead to wrinkle. The pupils will be dilated, eyes often wider than normal. The mouth might also hang open briefly. No matter if the surprise is positive or negative, the reaction tends to be exactly the same. It is one of the only emotions that can present itself this way, no matter the cause, which can be rather fascinating to think about.

Contempt

This is a feeling of disregard, and it is complex by nature. Contempt is almost always triggered by something beforehand. It is kind of unlikely to just begin feeling it out of nowhere. We don't all feel contempt on a regular basis. Those with accepting personality types will usually fall on a different emotion before ever reaching a state of contempt. This can be why it is so hard for us to understand one another. Imagine trying to see things from a different viewpoint that you have never felt before. If you are someone who does not personally experience contempt, the best thing to do is research it and be mindful of it when you see others going through it.

How We Express It: For such a strong emotion, the eyes are ironically hardly changed. In fact, there is normally a vacant look behind them. The lips might appear uneven during this time, with one corner pulled up and back. As mentioned, this emotion is one that can often overlap with others. Anger can evolve into contempt just as easily as distrust can follow contempt. Because it can be very confusing, the body will physically decide to be void of reaction in the moment.

Correlation

You now have a grasp of the most common human emotions, as well as the 16 main personality types. The next thing that you are probably wondering is how all of this fits together. It is a complex web of feelings that are set into motion by personality traits and actions that form due to natural instinct. Psychologists have been studying this correlation for many decades now, as it is a very fascinating topic to research. If you have one. You will come to find out that when you have one aspect figured out, you won't necessarily be able to predict others.

For example, if you have a friend that is direct and aggressive in personal situations, you might believe that he would also lash out at a boss or higher authority. Because so many other factors come into play, this friend might actually be very submissive and respectful when it comes to those in charge. This sets the stage for the age-old argument: are your actions fueled mostly by your personality or by the situations at hand? While this is no simple answer to this, both are actively involved. Depending on your personality type, you are going to be either more sensitive or less sensitive to situational issues than other people. Some of us prefer to act only after fully assessing a situation carefully.

There are other people who are rooted in their actions and choose to act before gathering all of the details. This also ties into the point that some people are more calculated and rely on logic while others go based off of instinct. Another interesting point to bring up is the fact that humans often gravitate toward what is familiar or comfortable. If you take a look at a naturally aggressive person, you will realize that he often puts himself in situations where he can win arguments. The same can also be said for quiet, passive individuals. You won't find a shy person willingly volunteering to get up on stage to be judged by other people. It takes outside factors to push someone out of their comfort zone. Humans are truly creatures of habit.

As you can see, this is why engaging with others that are different from yourself can often lead you to experiences that you would have never sought out for yourself. This is also true when it comes to the person that you are dating. Branching out is a healthy part of growing as a person. In children, we often encourage them to try new things, whether it be food, games, or sports. This doesn't need to stop just because we are adults. Pushing yourself to do something extreme can cause adverse effects, a general unwillingness to try. If you can find something that is reasonably within your comfort zone, given the proper push from someone else (or your willpower), then you will likely be able to accomplish it. People do this all the time with things that they are fearful of - roller coasters are an example.

As humans, we gravitate toward stable options. If you were walking around in the woods and you encountered a safe, clear path alongside a path that was draped in thorn bushes and snakes, the choice would be pretty clear. It is natural to want to feel safe. We all have different ways of protecting ourselves when we begin to feel threatened. This is where your personality comes shining through. A defense mechanism is an entirely unique way for you to protect your state of being. Some people will flee, others will speak up about the situation. No matter what you do, the main goal is the same — to be in a stable situation.

Behavior can be analyzed and predicted all day long, but something to remember is that no single person is going to display 100% consistent actions. Things happen and feelings come up that push us off of our intended path. This is what makes life so interesting. We all have slight variations of ourselves that tend to come through when we are feeling different emotions. Think about your favorite movie. If you are in a happy mood and your favorite movie comes on TV, you'll probably want to sit down and watch it. Now think about going through heartbreak; you likely won't be in the mood to watch a movie because of all the feelings that you are processing. In fact, seeing that the movie is on TV might be off-putting to you. Small things like this can change your behavior tremendously.

Chapter 8: Personality and Workplace

Your work environment is likely your most challenging environment to face. It is a place where many different personalities must come together in order to complete tasks. Likely being assigned responsibility, it is a guarantee that you have felt incredibly stressed at work before. During these situations, you will notice that there is a large possibility for a personality clash. Having that many different people working together can be a very complex situation. So, how can you ensure that you are doing a great job while also getting along with your coworkers?

<u>Start from Within</u>

Through the research that you have been doing, you should know all about your personality type by now. No one else is going to know how you operate better than you. When it comes to getting through your workload, you will know which conditions will stimulate your best work. Do you like to work chronologically? Do you listen to music while you work? Are you able to multitask? Considering all possibilities, you should make it a goal for yourself to work as comfortably as possible. Do anything that you can to make your work environment a comfortable and productive space. Many forget that there are little things that can be changed in order to promote productivity. Don't be afraid to reach out to your supervisor if need be. There is nothing wrong with wanting to enhance your productivity. Know your triggers — this is important. Everyone is triggered from time to time. This doesn't have to be as serious as it sounds, but know that it has the possibility to be. What do you do for yourself in these situations? Do you step away or do you engage? An example of some triggers will follow:

● Someone in the workplace is abusing his power, ordering other people around and not doing his fair share of work. This causes you to feel like you are not being properly recognized for your efforts, often working just to catch up. A very frustrating case, it happens a lot in the workplace. What You Can Do : If you ever feel that there is an unfair balance taking place, make sure that you speak up about it. Reach out to someone that works above you. If it is the boss that is making you feel this way, you might need to seek counsel from someone at an even higher position in the company. Know that you are allowed to value yourself and your worth. Being placed under these stressful working conditions can take a toll and might even cause some negative aspects of your personality to surface over time.

● Your coworker just won't stop pestering you, no matter what is going on. If you are in the middle of concentrating on something important, a disruption could be very detrimental to your progress. With most personality types, being interrupted can cause you to either lash out or feel very overwhelmed. The worst part is when the other person is unaware or simply inconsiderate of the impact that this can have on you. What You Can Do : While confrontation can be hard for some of us, it is sometimes essential. There is a misconception between confrontation and fighting, most of the time. A confrontation does not need to equal a screaming match. All it means is that you need to state your case clearly to the person that is causing you the disruption. Explain why their behavior bothers you and offer a solution that you can follow. Taking out any open-ended statements will allow you to resolve the situation after one conversation rather than having it drag on.

● After you get off of work each Friday, imagine that all of your coworkers get together for drinks and they never invite you. This is a different kind of trigger, one that revolves around more social aspects of the workplace. Situations like these are tricky because they don't revolve around a system of rules or guidelines. Socialization is something that is unique in itself, but it can still have the ability to do great emotional damage to your personality. This is especially true for those who are more introverted. What You Can Do : Asserting yourself is one of the most challenging aspects of being a human. If you are on the quiet side, it is unlikely that you are going to speak out about being left out. Instead, you can compromise. We all naturally form alliances, no matter how reserved we are. Human connection is important for getting through life. If you do wish to have a friendship with any of your coworkers, try asking them if they want to hang out off the clock. By creating a new social situation, you will have more control. The way that others perceive you is a very complex thing, as we have learned. After seeing that you take initiative in the social realm, others might see this as a cue that you do want to be invited to get drinks after all.

● If you are a caretaker, it is within your nature to make sure that others are alright. When you have a coworker that isn't pulling enough weight, you might have the urge to step in and help. This can turn out to be a very positive action, forming a bond with your coworkers. The thing that you must remember when you are helping others is that you cannot spread yourself too thin. If you start to lose quality in your own work because you are helping others complete theirs, then this is a problem. Knowing how to draw the line is an important boundary to learn. It can be harder for those with the natural instinct to want to help people. What You Can Do : Ask yourself if you are where you need to be in terms of progress. Is your workload on track? Is your work of the right quality? If you answered no to either of these, then you should think twice before jumping in and trying to save the day. While it can seem like you are turning your back on the person at first, you will realize that you can't successfully assist someone until you are on track with your own responsibilities. Balance is everything when you are dealing with your natural personality traits in the workplace.

● Think about your boss promising you a promotion for the last few months. You have been working hard to show your boss that you are deserving of this promotion, often staying late and working weekends to prove that you are devoted to the company. When the day finally rolls around, you realize that your coworker has been given the position instead. You are stuck with the struggle of not wanting to appear jealous but also wanted to stand up toward this injustice. The situation especially angers you because your coworker has not been as consistent as you have been. He has been calling in sick and late on his assignments. What You Can Do : Injustice is hard to face, and this is especially true in your workplace. Again, the way that you react in this situation is going to rely heavily on the type of personality that you have. This is another case where you must assert your ability to make a direct confrontation. Whether you naturally have this ability within, or you have to branch outside of your comfort zone, you should definitely speak up to your boss. Instead of bashing your coworker, you can explain to your boss why you believe that you are the right candidate for the position. Mention all of the ways that you were putting in additional effort.

These examples, although very different, all focus on one point — you need to know yourself well. Getting to know yourself can sound like a weird concept at first. You might think, of course you know who you are. Have you ever felt confused by your own actions? This is normal, and it happens more often than people will admit. Getting to know yourself is much more than knowing what you like to eat and watch on tv. It is a sense of how you operate, mentally. It is knowing why your personality drives you to do the things that you do. Getting to know yourself on this level does not happen over time. It can take months, or even years to get to this point. If you begin now, you will have an easier time deciphering your own actions.

A person who is on top of their own feelings and behaviors will have a much easier time processing them and moving forward. The reason why many find their workplace to be insufferable is often because they are feeling trapped. This feeling can come from disliking your line or work or from not getting along with your coworkers. It is a bad mental state to be in when you are expected to perform your best. While you cannot just leave your job in order to go soul-searching, there are ways for you to better understand yourself without having to change very much about your daily routine. Consider participating in the following activities that will open your mind to this kind of knowledge:

Meditation

Depending on how comfortable you are with silence, this can be a topic that brings up mixed emotions. A lot of people do not see the benefit of sitting around "doing nothing," but it can help you tremendously. Daily life is something that never seems to slow down. By participating in regular meditation, you are giving your brain the chance to rest without being asleep. Why is this beneficial? Thoughts that are prominent on your mind will tend to rise to the surface when you meditate. If you have been feeling agitated lately, lashing out at loved ones for seemingly no reason at all, you might find the cause through meditation. It does not have to be a long session. If you are a beginner, you can try laying down or sitting still for 10- minute intervals. The only thing you will need is a quiet place for you to be alone with your thoughts. Allow your mind to wander exactly where it naturally does. You might be surprised at the thoughts that come up.

<u>Journaling</u>

Most of us stopped journaling regularly after we left childhood. This is another very beneficial way to do some self-discovery. Journaling is similar to meditation, but it requires your brain to be a little bit more active. There aren't any rules when it comes to jotting down your thoughts. For the most effective results, try to sit alone in a quiet room for about 10-15 minutes to start. Put your pen to the page and write down the very first thought that comes to mind. If you don't know what to say, make a list of everything that you have done since you woke up. Simple exercises such as this will give your brain the stimulation that it needs. For some, it is easier to express things on paper than it is to another person.

Having these short records of your thoughts is a great way to learn more about your personality and behaviors. You can look back on your journal entries and try to determine your thought process. It is an interesting habit to form that only takes up a short amount of time in your day. Once you start, you might find solace in doing this regularly. Volunteering Stepping out of your daily routine and into an entirely different situation can be an eye-opening experience. When you seek out volunteer opportunities, think about what you have a passion for. You can help animals, children, or other adults that are in need. Not only is this a way to learn more about yourself and your natural instincts, but you are helping other people along the way.

Volunteering

is an extremely positive thing for anyone to do at least one in their life. Working with other people is a skill that you never want to stop improving. Being able to see a situation on someone else's level makes you an easier person to get along with. When you volunteer you are giving your time and your skills by choice. It is a way for you to perform a selfless action while also completing a task and having a larger purpose.

Improved Relationships

As you establish a true sense of who you are as a person, you will then be able to better understand your coworkers and superiors. Instead of having to figure out your own actions and another person's actions, you will be able to observe what is unfolding around you. Creating a harmonious dynamic with anybody can be a challenge, but it is an essential part to having a positive workplace. Your boss will surely appreciate the effort that you make when it comes to your interaction with your coworkers. A business cannot operate successfully if the people that are responsible for making it run find each other repulsive. Strive toward healthy relationships with all of your coworkers, even if you find that your personalities clash. You are not obligated to take the relationship outside of the professional setting, but if you do, then you will benefit by having another friend. These dynamics do not have to be complicated and stressful. As long as you set forth with your intention clearly, then others will recognize that and have a higher chance of respecting you. For those that are lacking in the self-confidence department, you can make up for this by choosing a cause that you wholeheartedly support. This can be workplace productivity or healthy leadership skills. No matter what you decide to focus on, you will succeed because of your efforts and concentration

Chapter 9: Personality and Parenting

Think about the way that you were raised. The things that you were or were not allowed to do as a child surely shaped the way that you behave now as an adult. We all know that temperament, personality, and habits all form rapidly when you are in your childhood years. Parenting can be one of the most difficult yet most rewarding tasks to accomplish. It can be insanely frustrating when you feel that you are doing your very best to provide for your child, only to realize that he is still acting out. Even during times like these, having a great understanding of the dynamic between your own personality and your child's can make all of the difference.

Try to Understand

As a parent, it might be instinctual to come up with an idea of what is "best" for your child, in your own opinion. So often we take charge as adults without thinking about the impacts and repercussions of our actions. The behavior that you display toward your child is what they are going to eventually learn as the "right" thing to do. Instead of forcing a set of behaviors on your child, try to understand the way that they naturally want to operate. While you do have to set boundaries and rules to keep him safe, you can also take some time to observe the way that he chooses to do things. This type of parenting is a different approach than a lot of the traditional methods that are used. By allowing the child his own freedom of choice, you are keeping his personality and temperament in mind.

Remember, these are things that already exist underneath the surface from the day that your child is born. While your actions do shape your child's personality, it is important to draw a line between trying to change them and helping them grow. Not allowing your child to indulge in cake before bedtime is an appropriate way to assert your boundaries. It makes sense and it does not change anything about his personality. It is simply a lesson that your child cannot always get what they want.

However, if your child wants to help you bake a cake to give to his grandmother, this is something you might want to explore. It is a snippet of his personality coming through, a caregiver type. It is not uncommon for children to want to return the caregiver role back to the adults who display it. This is a wonderful quality to have, and whenever possible, you should allow your child to explore it. Caring for other people promotes for a selfless personality. Of course, boundaries do have to be drawn if your child's well-being is at stake, but you will know when to step in if necessary.

Personality: The Child

As a parent, it might come naturally to wonder why your child acts out or misbehaves. You might feel that it is out of character to see this behavior on display. The truth is, the way that you choose to parent has a lot to do with the way that your child develops a personality. While your child can get your physical genes, it is actually a misconception that a child will get your emotional genes. The personality develops a lot within the first few years of life, making for a very impressionable mind. For example, if you revolve your parenting around avoiding the truth and telling small lies in order to curb behavior, your child will likely have trust issues that can be seen through personality traits. If you decide to take a controlling approach to your parenting, your child might end up rebelling in the future.

Those who believe in a strict form of parenting like this tend to raise children who have a need to act out. Parenting is all about balance, and if you think about it, the way that you speak to your child can have an impact on his personality. On the other end of the spectrum, your actions can positively impact your child. If you teach loving values, your child will likely grow up mimicking this behavior. A lot of parents don't realize how influential their own behavior can be when it comes to what their children absorb. Deciding on a parenting style can be one of the toughest decisions that you make. Consider this — treat your child as a small adult.

The bottom line is that you need to provide them with respect if you want the same respect in return. Teach them behavioral concepts that are easy to understand, but also mature in nature. If you treat your child like a baby, allowing them to get away with anything, you can expect the same behavior to continue as your child grows up. Of course, there is a fine line between giving your child respect and acting as a disciplinarian. While you don't want to approach this in a way that is too dominant, your child should still know that you are in charge and that you must be listened to. Your child might begin to display some unfavorable personality traits. Before you punish them for the behavior, consider which parenting techniques that you are currently utilizing. This could be an indication that it is time for a change.

Gentle parenting might work out for the first few years, but then a sterner approach might become necessary as your child's personality develops. Parenting is a lot of trial and error until you come to the right conclusion. Know that if your child begins to act out, this does not mean that you are a bad parent. As you have discovered, there are many different personality types that operate in unique ways. The same definitely applies to growing children.

Personality: The Parent

As a parent, when you are in the comfort of your own home, you might display a different side to your own personality. We all tend to be more relaxed when we are in a familiar environment. Think about the way that you would discipline your child in the grocery store compared to when you are at home. It is likely that your voice would be quieter and you would want to make less of a scene.

Essentially, you need to have a parenting style that can work well in public, as well as in private. It is important that you teach your child the difference between behaviors that might only be appropriate at home versus behaviors that will cause disruption when in public. A lot of parents dread taking their children out to restaurants or retail stores because of this dilemma. You might have a well-behaved child before you leave the house, only to experience the stress of a temper tantrum as soon as you arrive at your destination. On your end, you need to exercise a lot of patience. Your child will not be able to learn these things unless you teach them.

Depending on your own personality type, patience will either be very easy to come by or it will be a bit of a personal challenge. No matter what the case is, this will be something that you will be responsible for mastering. Being flexible is also an important personality trait to hold as a parent. You need to be able to go with the flow of things and be accepting if things do not go originally as planned. That is what parenting is all about, being able to cope with the unknown. Personality types do play a large role in the parenting style that is chosen. Types INFP, INTP, and ESFP are the caretakers of the personality types. They love to bring order to life and they will often be the personality types of stay-at-home parents. It is an interesting statistic to think about. All three share one thing in common, and that is the perceiving trait.

As a refresher, this type of individual is more okay with things that turn out to be spontaneous. They are able to operate under unknown circumstances while still feeling as if they are in control of their own lives. Externally, they are able to remain casual and they will often have the most energy out of all the personality types. As you know, this type of energy level will make parenting a lot easier.

In terms of having confidence as a parent, those with extroverted personality types think a lot more highly of themselves than those who are introverts. ESFJ and ESTJ both see their parenting skills as valuable. You can see here that the two personality types are very similar, only differing when it comes to the feeling and thinking aspects. Taking a look at another interesting statistic, it is said that personality types INTJ, ISTP, and ISTJ are among the top who say they do not have nor want children. Researchers believe that the introverted aspect of their personality types could have something to do with this conclusion. Those who are more reserved tend to feel nervous at the thought of being responsible for a child and all of the parenting that comes along with childhood. That isn't to say that these individuals would not make great parents, though. All three have some very valuable traits that would definitely come into play if they were to decide to have children.

In terms of those who are already most likely to have children, ESFJ and ESFP are at the top of the list. These are two very strong and very similar personality types. You will notice that both of them hold extroverted personality traits.

How to Improve Parenting

If you want to become a better parent to your child, one of the first steps is going to be internal. You must be able to identify who you are as a person and the level that you operate on. If it is difficult for you to understand yourself, then you can imagine how confused your child might become. Know what you value and what you are not okay with; starting with a strong foundation like this will allow you to come up with clear rules and guidelines that abide by this. Sending a child mixed information will never turn out well. It just becomes confusing and leaves room for distrust in the future. One of the best rules when it comes to parenting is to mean what you say and say what you do. If you intend on setting a punishment for behavior that you deem unacceptable, you need to stick to it. This creates a firm sense of discipline in your child's life. This structure becomes important as your child grows.

The same applies if you promise a reward. Following through with things is the easiest way to build trust and a sense of stability. Overcoming your ego is another important thing that you must do if you want to improve your parenting techniques. Raising a child can be incredibly frustrating and difficult at times. Being able to admit when you are wrong is important as an adult. You need to let your child know that you do make mistakes sometimes, and that it is okay to do so. Nobody is invincible, so make sure that you teach your child that from the very start. Having a decent perception of reality is going to be much better for your parenting than using techniques that are based on untrue circumstances. Children have a great grasp on things, as long as you are able to explain it to them clearly and concisely.

This can prove to be challenging for those with personality types that revolve around imaging abstract concepts. If you are not firmly rooted in reality, there will be hundreds of possibilities that can come up. It is great for a child to be able to engage their imagination, but making important decisions based on this logic will probably result in some adverse effects. If your child is struggling with your current parenting approach, you might just need to break down the concepts in a simpler fashion. Pushing too much information on a child can be overwhelming at times.

Certain personality types revolve around intricate thinking patterns. If you are one of these people, know that sometimes you might have to break things down in order for them to have an impact on your child. Try sticking to things that you know are essential to behavioral growth. If you find that one approach does not work, stop it entirely and try a different one. When you try too many at a single time, not only will this be ineffective, but it will also be difficult to tell which ones work and which ones do not. Children are keen on the way that you are feeling; they will be able to sense when you are frustrated or upset. This is when your own self-control will come into play. You should not censor yourself to the extent of lying to your child, but you should curb your behavior if you find that it is negatively impacting your child's behavior.

Chapter 10: How to Identify Personality Types

Now that you have spent all this time learning about the different personality types, you will probably want to put your knowledge to the test. Analyzing people can be an interesting experience. You will likely be able to easily recognize those with personality types that are similar to yours, and also those who act in a completely opposite way. Identifying what falls in the middle can be more challenging. There is a lot that can be observed if you are looking to classify someone's personality type. You can take a look at their physical traits, the way that they present themselves in a room, how they respond to stressful situations, how much they enjoy social interactions, and much more. Where do you even begin?

<u>Body Language</u>

You can learn a lot about a person if you study their non-verbal communication. As you know, emotions can be read on a person's face if you take a look at what their features are doing. A simple crossing of the arms can indicate a hostile approach, while a warm smile and open shoulders can say the exact opposite. When you are beginning to decipher a person's personality type, first take a look at what is not being said. These responses often happen naturally, so much that a person cannot censor them. Some people are very easy to read, wearing their emotions all over their face.

Others can do a better job of hiding them. The eyes will tell you most of what you need to know. Pay attention to the way that the eyebrows frame the eyes.

Are they raised or lowered? Are they wrinkled in concern or sadness? Most people, no matter how reserved they are, will do a lot of communicating behind their eyes. When you talk to the person, do they engage in direct eye contact? Do they look away frequently while they are talking to you? It is common for extroverts to enjoy prolonged eye contact while introverts are uncomfortable with the idea of it.

Extroverts will also likely be more exaggerated with their non-verbal cues while introverts prefer to be a little bit more on the pensive side. The hands can also say a lot about a person. What is the person doing with their hands? Are they nervously fidgeting? Are they placing their hands strongly on their hips? This action can clue you in to how the individual is feeling about the given situation. During times of stress, some people choose to wring their hands in order to relieve some of the tension. You might have also noticed that when a person gets really angry, their fists naturally begin to ball up.

Another way that you can assess behavior comes through a handshake. Take note of whether the handshake is firm or soft. Those with more self-confidence will likely have a firmer handshake. These individuals will also likely make direct eye contact with you as you shake hands. Extroverts will normally talk with their hands a lot. Because they have the need to make larger gestures and exaggerated points, utilizing the hands while talking can be an additional form of self-expression. If you have never taken notice of the placement of someone's hands, you will probably find it very interesting when you start to. When you take a look at someone, observe how they are standing. Is their body directly facing you? Are they turned away? Are their shoulders broad and open or are they more closed off? All of these factors can indicate something about personality traits.

If someone is uncomfortable in a situation, they will likely have one of two responses — they will become smaller or they will try to appear larger. This is the flight-or-flight response in action. Making yourself seem larger than what is making you uncomfortable is a primitive action that humans have been doing for centuries. It can provide a sense of security, even when the person isn't feeling the most confident. If something is not pleasing to a person, their stance might reflect this by becoming more closed off or dismissive. When something is not as exciting or appealing, the body tends to relax more. This action can be a dead giveaway to boredom or contempt.

Responses

Take note of how fast someone responds to a question. This can be a big clue to identifying what type of personality you are dealing with. Does the person respond right away, seemingly before thinking about all of the options through? Is there a slight pause, a moment of hesitation before coming to a final conclusion? Those who need to take a little bit of extra time are most likely introverts. If you have ever noticed someone talking through all of the different options aloud, this is likely someone who is an extroverted personality that is ruled by judgment. Using logic to come to this point is going to make a lot of sense for a person with these traits. Another thing that you might notice is a person's decision to respond first or last. If it comes down to group discussion, an extrovert will likely have no problem being the first to respond, even when others are waiting.

Because an introvert does require a little bit more time to think, they will usually respond last. The language that is used during a response is something to also pay attention to. Those with logical brains normally speak as though what they are saying is something factual. Because of the consideration that they have already taken, they will have the confidence to approach things from a factual point of view. Others might express that their answer is simply a "what if," or a theory. Abstract thinkers love to rely on their imagination in order to come to a conclusion. Of course, there are also personality types that rely on a little bit of both when they respond to a question. Critical thinkers love to provide long responses. They like to review information and go over concepts with other people. When someone is thinking based on concepts rather than facts, they might provide incomplete statements when they decide to respond.

Mindfulness

A way that you can gauge someone's thinking or feeling personality traits comes in the way that they make decisions. Does the individual consider how others might be affected by their decision? Those who are of the feeling type are definitely considerate of how other people are going to react to the outcome. Even if it is a decision that is of a personal nature, your typical feeling type is still going to consider other people before coming to a final conclusion. This type of selflessness can be a great quality to have. After all, putting others first is a brave thing to do. It can cross the line into being detrimental, though. With little regard for oneself, the feeling type might make decisions that are solely based on the well-being of others. It takes balance in order to achieve the right mix of considerate and practical.

The thinking type believes that whatever happens, happens. This individual is likely going to see that if they must adapt to a situation, then others should have no problem adapting to it as well. This does not mean that thinkers lack consideration, but instead, their priorities are a bit different. They tend to see things as very black and white — a problem with a solution. There is normally no room for them to participate in any grey-area thinking. These individuals will likely be very direct when they communicate, not trying to spare any feelings. Again, this isn't because they are naturally mean, but they just believe in saying things how they appear. Of course, some people can show a mix of the two qualities. Judging by the charts in the earlier chapter, you can see that some personality types can overlap in traits. Do your best to judge immediate, first reactions from people. The very first gut instinct will normally tell you the most about a person that you are trying to figure out.

The same rule can also apply to your own behavior if you are trying to analyze yourself. Consider what your first instinct is during any given situation. Are you thinking about the outcome and how it will affect others or the outcome and how it will affect yourself? Does the thought of how other people will handle it cause you any worry? Are you able to come to the conclusion easily, without any guilt on your conscience?

Change

We all have fairly unique responses when it comes to the topic of change. This is so because change is normally outside of our control. A sudden change and the reaction to it can tell you a lot about a person. There are normally a few responses: the person has no problem with the change and is able to continue on normally, the person resists the change and suggests other alternatives or the person is uncomfortable with the change and it causes distress. Where do you fit in on this spectrum? A perceiving type is likely going to be uncomfortable with change. This individual likes to be in control of the situation, so you will probably see them throw out other suggestions. He might feel upset or offended if other people do not take his suggestions.

A judging type does not like going back on plans that are already seemingly set in stone. This individual will likely push for the original plan, explaining that it doesn't make sense to change it now. This is actually a defense mechanism to hide that he is uncomfortable with the way that the situation is unfolding. On the other hand, a judging type might also go along with the change and suffer in silence, not wanting to call attention to the fact that he cannot handle it. This type of person will consider many different options, but once something has been decided on, the individual will not want any other changes to occur. This is an interesting example of personality types to consider. It also explains a lot when it comes to conflict resolution.

Have you ever been in a fight with someone who is getting all worked up over what is seemingly nothing? You can see how some people hold onto things while others have the ability to let go and go with the flow. It all comes down to the way that we are wired, and without any type of resolution, you are likely going to butt heads with those who feel differently. Know that this is something that a person cannot easily change. Take yourself as an example. How do you feel about change? If someone were to tell you to feel the opposite way about a situation, would you be able to do so in an instant? Probably not. Becoming a more tolerant person is something that you can do to make things a little bit easier.

How to Classify Personality and Temperament

By now, you should be very familiar with not only the different personality types but also the different temperament types. The two can actually be grouped together and categorized into 4 additional types that will assist you for when you are trying to identify how someone operates. These types are Golds, Reds, Greens, and Blues. Below is a breakdown of the traits that are found in each one:

Golds

People who see events that happen in the present as building blocks toward the future are classified as Golds. This is normally a sensing/judging personality type. These individuals do not typically enjoy change and will do everything in their power to stay on a consistent schedule. They take it upon themselves to ensure that everything is in working order, from family life to work responsibilities. Guardian is the role that they like to take on, providing for other people.

Reds

These individuals take on an Artisan role. A more erratic personality type, Reds love to take on several little problems at once. Instead of focusing on one thing at a time, this individual is able to multitask, which can serve as both a blessing and a curse. When it comes to problem-solving, Reds would rather figure things out immediately than spend another minute with something unsolved. This is a sensing/perceiving type of individual. People that fall under this category normally will not create a master plan for getting things done. Instead, they seem to take things head-on.

Greens

This personality type is one of the steadiest that you will find. They enjoy thinking logically while also incorporating reasoning skills into the mix. They have a lot of patience, more than most people. Doing a great job of prioritizing their time, Greens will ensure that they know how to divide up their responsibilities. For this reason, you will see that Greens are likely going to be great workers in almost any field. They also make great students with a keen ability to study and keep up with schoolwork. Believing that there is always a systematic way to handle any situation, you will see this personality type utilizing their methods both in personal and professional life.

Blues

This type has the strongest conscience of all 4. An individual who falls under this category will most likely rely a lot on their sense of intuition to figure out predicaments. In order to know that they are making the best decision possible, this individual will stop and think about all of the possibilities (both realistic and abstract) in order to make the right choice. They value a true sense of authenticity and prefer to only interact with others that can show the same in return. This is a more sensitive type of person, one that tends to focus inward in times of great importance.

Chapter 11: How to Change Your Personality

Self-improvement is a great thing to focus on. It can allow you to learn more about yourself while also improving your positive traits. Many people have the desire to change, but when it all comes down to it, they don't take any steps in the right direction. Remember, your personality is something that you are born with. While you can't do away with it forever, you can definitely learn some alternative behaviors to the ones that you would like to get rid of. Focusing on this change will not only make an impact on your life, but it might also influence those who are around you. Nobody enjoys being around a person who is miserable, so if you feel that your personality could use a bit of sprucing up, consider the following tips for making the change.

Make Realistic Changes

Know that when "changing" your personality, what you are really striving for is an improvement. Making long-lasting changes is nearly impossible, especially since you have gotten to this point in your life with the same personality. Curbing certain behavior is possible, but it does take a certain amount of work. Knowing that you are going in to make improvements rather than to change who you are entirely is going to help you a lot. Those who think that they can completely change themselves, or even others, end up becoming a lot more disappointed when they realize that it isn't possible. This comes up a lot in relationships.

Perhaps you have been in a situation where you love somebody but their behavior is unfavorable. You might have believed that you could change them for the better, providing nothing but positive examples and guiding them in the right direction. While this would surely help, when it comes down to it, we are all pretty rooted in our original personality traits. You should not be discouraged when it comes to changing your own personality. Nobody knows you better than you know yourself, so it makes sense that you would be able to guide yourself through these changes.

As long as you remain realistic during the process, you should be able to see some noticeable improvements. For example, if you stay up really late into the night watching TV and eating, this is a habit that you can change. Becoming a morning person who operates better during daylight hours will be difficult, but it can definitely change an aspect of your personality. In order to do this, you will need to rely on your willpower and your selfdiscipline. This is a realistic approach to changing a certain aspect of your personality for the better. With this additional rest, you will be able to accomplish more during the day. You will also likely sleep better because you will not be eating large amounts of food at odd hours. Staying on track of changes becomes a lot easier when you make them attainable for yourself.

Consider the Factors

Depending on what you'd like to change about yourself, you will have to consider the factors that come into play that trigger the behavior. These factors can be environmental, social, or even physical. Most of the time, changing up the environment will do a lot when you have the desire to change your behavior. Without us even realizing it, the environment has a lot to do with the way that we act. The good news is, most of the time, the environment can be controlled. Imagine that you are waiting in line at a grocery store. You can feel yourself getting impatient, and by the time you finally reach the cashier, you snap at her because of your frustration.

This is something that you can definitely work on. Instead of directing your anger toward other people, think about why you are getting angry. There might be a lot of noise and other people surrounding you. Maybe someone cut in line, causing you to have to wait even longer. While these things are irritating, they are not the cashier's fault. Being able to think clearly and rationally could help you from lashing out at other people who don't deserve it. To combat this, maybe you could work on breathing exercises. Distractions, such as playing games on your phone, might also help you while you wait in line. There is always a better alternative if you have the patience to seek it.

As mentioned, you can change your environment in order to curb your behavior. Maybe you can go grocery shopping earlier or later in the day in order to avoid busy times. You can also decide to go into a different, smaller store if you want to avoid the crowds. There are plenty of options for you to still achieve the same goal of buying groceries. Most problems can be fixed with a similar solution. As long as you are able to determine what is causing you distress, you should also be able to come up with some solutions for how to change it.

Another example would be if you were to lose your patience easily with your significant other. Maybe you are having a normal conversation and then you come to the point where you disagree with an opinion. Instead of turning this into a full-blown fight, you can learn to set aside your differences. This can happen by listening to what your partner has to say, expressing your opinion, and then moving forward. A big factor that makes a lot of people intolerant to change is the inability to progress. Most of us stay stuck on certain issues for far too long. Being able to let go of things sounds admittedly easier than it actually is. If you are looking to change this aspect of your personality, you can work on it by remaining calm and working through problems before frustration takes over.

Break Bad Habits

What defines a bad habit? We all have them, but we might disagree on what fits the description. In terms of your personality, a bad habit is anything that triggers you into making a negative response. Expressing your feelings is an important thing, but doing so in a healthy way can make all of the difference. If you are trying to become a more open-minded person, you should analyze your own behavior. What are some habits that you notice in your daily routine? Maybe you are intolerant to change.

Another way to identify these habits is by asking someone who is close to you. A person with a third-party view might be very eye-opening for you to speak with regarding your own behavior. There are things that you might never realize that you do until they are brought to your attention by other people. Nobody is perfect, and we all have habits that could probably do with being changed. Forming a new habit can take a lot of time, so don't be discouraged with yourself for continuing with the old one. A habit might be something that you learned in childhood, and that can mean several years of displaying the same behavior. It becomes second nature at a certain point.

As adults, we really need to make an effort if we would like to see a change in our own behavior. Setting goals for yourself can prove to be very rewarding once you start to notice the change. Don't give up, and surround yourself with people who are going to support you. You might have to consider who you are spending the most time with. If you notice that your efforts aren't making much of a difference, maybe you are being influenced by some outside sources. Even if you are a kind, caring person, hanging out with people who are incredibly selfish will eventually start to impact you negatively. Whether they stress you out or end up teaching you bad habits, it is probably best to steer clear of those who do not have anything positive to add to your life. This can be a very hard decision to make, and it could potentially cause some rifts. If something is important to you, though, you will be willing to make the sacrifice.

Surround Yourself with Good People

When we learn something new, it is often that we are most responsive to live examples. The same can be said when it comes to personality traits and behavioral habits. Being around people that you would like to be like is a good way to encourage new behaviors. As mentioned, if you are around a bunch of inconsiderate people, it is likely that this behavior will rub off on you. Surround yourself with people that possess the traits that you are trying to strive for. It can also be good to have a mentor of sorts. This can take away a lot of the stress that comes from trying to understand different personality types. If you have someone who is dedicated to helping you become the best version of yourself that you can be, it is like the weight of the task can be divided between the two of you.

A mentor can be anyone that you deed worthy. It does not necessarily have to be an older family member or a therapist (those are fine choices if you decide on them, though). Think about your friend group. Is there anyone that you admire when it comes to having amazing personality traits? Try to spend more one-on-one time with this individual. Be open to having meaningful conversations. The more that you open your mind, the more likely you will be to pick up on some of these habits. Don't be afraid to ask questions and ask for help.

Maybe you have a bad habit of interrupting people. By telling your mentor this, you now have two people to hold you accountable. If you don't want your mentor to be someone that you already know, there are many support groups that you can join. Self-betterment is not a topic of rarity. So many people strive for this same goal on a daily basis. Through a support group, not only will you get to meet some of these people, but you will be able to share your experiences with people who are going to be able to relate to you. As time goes on, you might even be able to fill the mentor role for someone else.

Conclusion

If one thing is for certain, it can be hard to accurately describe a personality. Whether it be your own personality or someone else's, these behaviors are made up of unique traits that form over time. Your personality is like the backbone to who you are as a person. It gives others an idea of who you are, and it allows you to study why you act the way that you do. Analyzing yourself can often be a stressful experience, but given the different personality tests that you can take, you would probably be surprised at your findings. Made up of 4 letter acronyms, each of the 16 personality types will paint a different picture in your head. You have introvert/extrovert, sensing/intuition, feeling/thinking, and judging/perceiving. These are the components that make up a personality.

Of course, temperament also plays a role in behavior. Your temperament begins to develop from the moment that you are born. You can be quiet and sweet, unsettled and fussy. As you grow older, this will also develop into something that is more substantial. Of all the different temperament types, there are 4 main ones that people tend to fall under: Sanguine, Phlegmatic, Choleric, and Melancholy.

Thinking about the bigger picture, an individual has a personality type and temperament type — this leaves room for so many different combinations of behaviors and habits. The interesting part of this all is that each person is born with a certain set of traits. On top of all this, sensitivity levels will come into play. These are fairly straight forward, you are either sensitive or you aren't. While it is a simple concept, being sensitive can do a lot for your behaviors that are already established. A sensitive introvert might have trouble communicating with other people in a large group. A sensitive extrovert might feel empathy for each person that he meets. This can all vary depending on the person, the situation, and the environment. It can be a lot of information to think about when you are trying to get a better sense of someone's personality.

Impacts of Personality

In any given situation, our personalities have the chance to shine through. This includes at the workplace, in a romantic relationship, and even as a parent. All of these instances require us to make decisions and take action. The way that you operate has a lot to do with your personality type. You might find that your personality makes work harder because you like to rely on your intuition while others gravitate toward logic. Maybe your partner enjoys going out on the weekends, but you would rather stay in and watch movies. When your child is giving you a hard time, you tend to give in because you get overwhelmed when you have to make decisions on the spot. These are all examples of normal life events that are driven by your personality type. To better understand how it all works, you must start by having a firm grasp on your own personality. Take some time to participate in self-care.

As mentioned, things like meditation and journaling can allow you to open your mind when you are trying to learn about these parts of yourself. It can be easier to pass judgment on others, but if you don't understand the source of your own behaviors first, then it makes no sense to analyze other people. Don't be afraid to question yourself; ask yourself why you do the things that you do. After studying your behavior for a little while, you might begin to see patterns and the roots of some traits. Having an understanding of the way that you operate will make it easier to make changes if need be.

Getting to the point where you realize that you are only human, and you do make mistakes, is a humbling experience. If there is something about your behavior that you feel is negative, you can work on changing this. Not only will you feel better about yourself, but people in your life will begin to notice, too. It takes a lot to work on yourself without being asked to do so first. There is a lot of power that can be felt in making the decision on your own and then successfully curbing your behavior. Think about the ways that you can improve your personality right now. These are attainable goals that you can strive for.

Understanding Others

Using the same form of analysis, you can study other people in order to better understand them. This doesn't have to be in depth; all you must do is use your observational skills. Once you know more about the different personality types, it will become easier to assign people to them. You likely already know a lot about introverted and extroverted behavior. This is one of the easiest traits to define. Pay attention to people in social settings.

When you are trying to understand a particular individual, take note on the level of participation that is happening. Is this person the first to speak or the last? Do they speak with confidence or are they on the quiet side? Do they enjoy standing in a crowd or would they rather be in a smaller circle? All of these things can help you define that aspect of the personality. Once you are more comfortable with identifying the other traits, you will be able to apply the same principle. Figuring people out is not as hard as it seems, as long as you are able to break down the behaviors.

Keep in mind that some people are also more open than others. Some are like open books, expressive and bold about the way that they present themselves. Others might take a little more time to figure out, only feeling comfortable once trust has been formed. The key to this is having patience. You will need to rely on your patience a lot when you are reading someone's personality. Just because you can't crack the code right away does not mean that it is impossible. Talk to people. Really try to get an understanding for the way that they think.

A common mistake that people make when trying to observe personality types is being too rigid in communication. Be genuine with what you say, the more natural the better. Nobody wants to have a conversation in which they feel like they are being interrogated. Getting to know someone in an authentic way can be a great, informative experience. It will also allow you to see things from another point of view, which is extremely important. Being able to coexist while having different viewpoints is one of the hardest things for people to learn. By expanding your mind to realize that you can still get along with those who have differing opinions can change your life. It brings along the mental maturity that is needed to have a healthy sense of emotional intelligence.

If you have ever wondered why your partner is very offended by something that does not seem like a big deal to you, working on this skill can improve your relationship. Even those who have grown up in the same environment can have very different behavioral traits. It is unfair to expect everyone to experience life the exact same way that you do. Be patient and mindful when dealing with others and you will likely be treated the same way in return.

Applying Change

Think about your personality as a trait that was assigned to you at birth, much like your eye color. While there are many ways that you can enhance your eyes with makeup and contact lenses, the true color remains underneath. This is the way that you are able to change your personality. The foundation is always going to be there. As children, we do not have control over how our brains develop. We rely on what is taught to us and on the environment that we are placed in. If you had a terrible childhood that was filled with a lot of trauma, you are going to have to work extra hard in order to make any changes. This is to no fault of your own, but it is something to consider when you set your personality goals.

The same can be said of a person who was raised in a strict, but loving, home. If you are trying to rid yourself of these rigid constructs as an adult, you will have to work hard to curb what you went through in childhood. The study of what happens in childhood and how it impacts us as adults is among the top psychological topics. Children have the most impressionable minds and are very eager to learn new things. What we were taught when we were little will likely keep coming up today as we navigate through the world as adults.

Change is possible, though. As long as you can keep your pre-existing factors in mind, you should be able to set some goals for yourself in terms of curbing your own behavior. When it comes to changing your own personality, this can be a very healthy step to becoming a better person. Remember, you cannot change other people. They will have to want to change, and if this is the case, you can help them along the way. No single person has the power to change you, though. By working to control your reactions, modify your habits, and place yourself in a healthier environment, you will be able to alter certain aspects of your own personality.

As long as you are willing to put in the work toward becoming a better person, then you are striving for a healthy goal. Combining all of the skills that you have learned regarding personality types and emotional intelligence will take the stress out of dealing with others and yourself. Remember, people are like puzzles. But as long as you have all of the right pieces, you will be able to figure things out.

www.ingramcontent.com/pod-product-compliance
Lightning Source LLC
Chambersburg PA
CBHW072108180226
39841CB00043B/1236